THE DEVOTIONAL POEMS OF MĪRĀBĀĪ

The Devotional Poems of Mīrābāī

Translated with Introduction and Notes

A. J. ALSTON

MOTILAL BANARSIDASS
Delhi :: Varanasi :: Patna

Indological Publishers & Booksellers
Head Office : Bungalow Road, Jawahar Nagar, Delhi-7
Branches : 1. Chowk, Varanasi-1 (U.P.)
2. Ashok Rajpath, Patna-4 (Bihar)

ISBN : 0-89581-510-9
LC No. : 81-900946

First Edition: *Delhi*, 1980
Price : Rs. 45 Cloth
Rs. 30 Paper

Printed in India
By Shantilal Jain, at Shri Jainendra Press, A-45, Phase-I,
Industrial Area, Naraina, New Delhi-110 028,
Published by Narendra Prakash Jain, for Motilal Banarsidass,
Bungalow Road, Jawahar Nagar, Delhi-110 007.

Most reverently
dedicated to my Teacher
Hari Prasād Shāstrī

PREFACE

The present work is intended to offer the reader a fair anthology of Mīrābāī's devotional songs, using for this purpose, with only slight departures, the fifteenth edition of Āchārya Parashurām Chaturvedī's well-known selection. The translation is intended to be faithful but readable. Notes are given at the back, filling out briefly the references in the poems to Hindu mythology and tradition that might not be familiar to the non-Hindu reader mentioning such readings adopted as differ from Shrī Chaturvedī's text, and discussing problematical points of interpretation. An Introduction is prefixed, containing three separate essays. The first deals with Mīrā's life. The second sketches in the rise and development of the Bhakti movement and tries to indicate Mīrā's place in it. The third discusses briefly the literary form and spiritual content of Mīrā's Padāvalī.

The work is addressed to the general reader rather than the specialist. In the Introduction and translation, full transliteration of Hindī and Sanskrit words and names has not been applied except in quoted phrases, but the long vowels ā, ī and ū have been marked as such throughout. Final short a has usually been dropped in these sections where this seemed appropriate according to modern spoken usage. Hindī and Sanskrit names and words, including the names of modern scholars, have in principle been transliterated in full throughout the Notes, where a greater degree of precision seemed required. Though this has sometimes resulted in the same word or name being spelt differently in different parts of the book, it should not cause serious inconvenience. The familiar "Mīrā" has been retained, though no doubt Mīrāṃ is the more correct form of the poetess's name. It must be admitted that perfect consistency in spelling has neither been sought nor achieved. Alternations between "You" and "Thou" in addressing the deity occur occasionally in the same poem, but not in the same sentence.

The author, not being himself a specialist either in the Rājasthānī dialect or the study of mediaeval Hindī texts, has had to rely on secondary sources both for the interpretation of

Mīrā's text and for most of the information contained in the introductory essays. The literature on Mīrā is now considerable, especially if account be taken of the work in learned periodicals and in languages other than Hindī. The author has not attempted to master all this vast range of material but has tried to make as intelligent use as he could of a few standard authorities such as P. Chaturvedī, Padmāvatī "Shabnam" and Bhuvaneshvara Nāth Mishra, and, for the wider background, H.P. Dvivedī, Ch. Vaudeville and S.K. De. In regard to the interpretation of the text, besides the Notes of Shrī Chaturvedī, the ṭikās of Y.N. Sharmā and T. Ṭaṇḍan, of D.S. Bhāṭī and of K.D. Sharmā were all invaluable. But on especially knotty points particular regard was paid to the Mīrān Kosh of Dr. Shashi Prabhā, as it seemed that the discipline of constructing a grammar and word-for-word dictionary of Shrī Chaturvedī's text must have given her the best chance of coming up with the right solutions. (See e.g. Notes 72, 90, 91, 94, 116, 119, 122, 147, 166, 167, 170, 176, 183) Thus the work is chiefly based on Indian authorities. And it is hoped that, if not a work of scholarship itself, it at least registers and brings before the English reader a part of the results of the work of Indian scholars on Mīrā in the past few decades.

My deepest debts are to my revered spiritual Teacher, the late Hari Prasād Shāstrī, founder of Shanti Sadan, London, who inspired all his pupils with a love of the mystical poetry of mediaeval India, while at the same time demonstrating in his own life that the practical teachings it conveys can still be applied and are fully relevant to the needs of the present day. My obligations to scholars are indicated above and acknowledged at appropriate points throughout the Introduction and Notes. I am obliged to the Librarian and staff of the Library of the School of Oriental and African Studies, London University, for the use of facilities and loan of books. I am extremely indebted to my wife for finding time *inter alia* to type the manuscript. I am very sorry that it is now too late to thank the late Mr. Sundarlal Jain, the distinguished Indological publisher, without whose encouragement the present book would not have appeared.

LONDON A. J. ALSTON

CONTENTS

INTRODUCTION

Mīrā's Life

The sketch of the life of Mīrā Bāī here presented is tentative. Like most modern accounts, it stems ultimately from the work of Munshī Devī Prasād entitled "Mīrāṃ Bāī kā Jīvan-Charitra", originally published in 1905. But it incorporates modifications of Devī Prasād's view, deriving from Āchārya Parashurām Chaturvedī, M.M. Gaurīshankar Hīrāchand Ojhā, Hermann Goetz and other authorities. In her work entitled "Mīrān: Vyaktitva aur Krititva", Padmāvatī "Shabnam" has set out the sources from which Mīrā's biography has been gradually built up, and has reviewed and critically examined the main efforts that have been made to reduce them to an intelligible whole. She concludes that Munshī Devī Prasād's theory is radically untenable at every point, and is not to be saved by mere minor modifications. It does indeed appear from her account that Devī Prasād's theory of the life of Mīrā is really no more than an imaginative construction, an attempt to reconcile data about Mīrā's birth and marriage that he found in the Archives of Mewār (Maḥkamah-e-Tavārīkh, Mewār) with the few facts that are known about the history of the Rājpūts at the time, the data available in the poetry that has come down in Mīrā's name, and the data in the later hagiographical literature. For his account of Mīrā's death he was partly dependent on the word of a court-minstrel whom he consulted and who claimed to be in possession of the correct tradition, though other traditions have been shown to exist with equal claims. Padmāvatī "Shabnam" certainly shows that the result was in many ways a weak and flimsy structure. But it was at least based on *some* documentary evidence, and it seems worth presenting the reader with some version of Devī Prasād's theory, as it is still the "consensus" view of modern Indian scholarship.

According to the consensus view, then, Mīrā was born about 1498 A.D. as the only daughter of Ratna Singh, a Rājpūt noble of the House of Rāthor. Her birth took place in a village in the neighbourhood of Mertā, a small fortress-city some forty or fifty miles north-east of the city of Ajmeer, itself about 220 miles south-west of Delhi. Her mother died when she was still very young, and since her father was much occupied with fighting, she was sent to live with her grandfather Rāu Dūdā jī in the palace of Mertā, the city he had himself taken from the Muslims and peopled with Hindus in 1461. Here she is said to have been educated in company with her cousin Jaymal, the future Rājpūt hero.

Mīrā appears to have been born in circumstances that favoured devotion to Krishna. There is a tradition that even before her mother died Mīrā had begged for, and ultimately received, an image of Krishna that had been in the possession of a holy man who visited her home. And there is a further tradition that she became so attached to the image that her mother jokingly told her that Krishna would be her bridegroom. Mīrā asks in one of her poems, "O Krishna, did You ever rightly value my childhood love?"(Poem 100) And she records (Poem 27) seeing herself married to the Lord in a dream. (Chaturvedī, Mīrāṃbāī Padāvalī p. 19). It is likely that Mīrā's devotion to Krishna was able to mature quickly during her time in the palace of her grandfather. It has been thought that Mīrā's life as an active devotee may well have set in here, with regular worship (pūjā) of the Lord embodied in an image, application of tilak to the brow, ceremonial waving of lights (āratī) and so forth. Rāu Dūdā jī, his eldest son, Mīrā's uncle Vīram jī, and Vīram jī's son Jaymal are all mentioned as devotees in the later hagiographical literature. It has been asserted on the basis of a reference to "a copper plate" that she was educated in the Vedas, Purāṇas and Upanishads by a Purohita called Gajādhara, who later accompanied her to her husband's home at the time of her marriage. (Bhuvaneśvara Nātha Miśra, p. 44). An education in Sanskrit as well as in music and dancing would not have been out of place in a Rājpūt princess of Mīrā's day.

In course of time, probably not long before 1516, Rāu Dūdā jī died. Mīrā's father Ratna Singh was still much away engaged in fighting, and her uncle Vīram jī assumed responsibility for her education and welfare when he succeeded to his father's kingdom. Meanwhile in 1508 the great warrior Rānā Sānga of the House of Sisodiyā had succeeded his father Rāymal to the Kingdom of Mewār, and ruled at Chittaur, the fortress that lay nearly 150 miles to the south of Mertā, across the Aravalli Hills. He was the acknowledged leader of the Rājpūts, and their best hope for unity in facing the challenge of the Muslim powers that already hemmed them in on all sides and were soon to be augmented by the arrival of Bābur. In 1516 Rānā Sāngā sought to cement his position by marriage alliances. He married Dhān Bāī, of the Jodhpur branch of the House of Rāthor, which ruled beyond his north-east boundaries. He arranged with Vīram Dev for the marriage of Mīrā with his own heir apparent, Prince Bhoja Rāj, thereby securing the allegiance of the power immediately to his north. And he entered into a marriage alliance with the power on his north-west border by marrying Karmavatī Bāī, sister of Hare Rāu, King of Būndī. It was this last alignment that boded ill for Mīrā. For fifteen years later, in 1531, when Rānā Sāngā had been dead over three years, Karmavatī's son Vikramājīta (or Vikramāditya) acceeded to the Kingdom of Mewār as a turbulent boy of fourteen, and Mīrā was exposed to the spite of the members of a rival house.

But this lay in the future. In 1516 Mīrā was married to Prince Bhoja Rāj, and from the fact that she was considered a suitable match for the heir-apparent at the most important capital of the Rājpūts it would be concluded that her religious devotion had not yet led her to behave in any way that contradicted family customs. The Sisodiyās, like the Rāthors, were "Vaishnavas" or worshippers of Vishnu, in practice chiefly of His incarnation as Krishna. Rānā Sāngā's grandfather, Rānā Kumbhā, had been a noted devotee. And there is a view (Goetz, p. 11) that the "Jhālī Rānī", the Rājpūt queen mentioned in the devotional literature as a pupil of the low-caste Guru Raidās, was none other than Ratan Kunwarī, mother of Rānā Sāngā. If this is true, and if the Jhālī Rānī were still dominating the women's side of the court at Chittaur in Mīrā's time, it might help to account for the fact that in four surviving poems she speaks of Raidās as her *Guru*, and also for the fact that many of her poems are coloured by the imagery and technical terminology of the "Sant" school to which he belonged. But it would not entitle us to think of Raidās as Mīrā's personal Guru. For he is believed to have taught in the middle of the fifteenth century, well before Mīrā was born. He is also said to have passed all his life in the neighbourhood of Banāras. It is believed by some that the Jhālī Rānī heard of his fame and had the power and influence to organize a considerable expedition to travel to Banāras to see him. Those who hold this view are easily able to explain Mīrā's persecution. They say that the Jhālī Rānī initiated her into the habit of receiving sādhus of the Sant school as visitors to enjoy their sat-sang. And then Mīrā continued with the practice after the Jhālī Rānī died or lost influence, thereby exposing herself to the charge of contradicting family custom.

Be all that as it may, the historians tell us that Mīrā was married to Bhoja Rāj in 1516, but that the marriage was childless and that her husband had already died before the death of Rānā Sāngā in January 1528. In her poems, Mīrā speaks of herself as a virgin. (Poems 51 and 77) The year 1527 was fateful for Mīrā. Rānā Sāngā assembled a great force of Rājpūts to oppose the invader Bābur, who possessed a smaller but well-drilled army, disposing of cannon. The Rājpūts suffered a terrible defeat at Khānua or Kanwāha, a village a few miles west of Āgrā, not far from Fatehpur Sīkrī. Mīrā's father Ratna Singh was killed, and Rānā Sāngā received grievous injuries. It is said that in January 1528 this heroic man was poisoned by some of his ministers to prevent him organizing a counter-attack on Bābur which would have resulted in many further casualties. (Goetz p. 18, Padmāvatī, p.99)

According to an arrangement made five years earlier, the boy Ratna Singh succeeded to the Kingdom. He was the son of Dhān Bāī, but Queen Karmavatī had a prominent place in the regency, (Goetz p. 12 f.) Though Ratna Singh's mother was a member of the Jodhpur branch of the Rāthor family, there was no sympathy in court circles for the Mertā branch, and an expedition was sent to attack Mīrā's uncle, Vīram Dev, ruling in Mertā. It is plausible to maintain that this was the beginning of a period of isolation for Mīrā, which drove her to make a final and complete rejection of the values of the society in which she was brought up. (Chaturvedī, Padāvalī p. 21) The poems suggest that, not content with receiving sādhus in the women's quarter at the palace, she began to sally forth to the temple in the town, mingle with the holy men there and dance before the image. (Poems 17, 19, 21) According to one of the reports found in the Archives of Mewar, it was already under the rulership of Ratna Singh that the persecution of Mīrā began. However, he was killed in a scuffle in 1531, and this left the way open for the installation of Queen Karmavatī's son Vikramājīta as Rānā, at that time a turbulent youth of fourteen or fifteen. A report found by Munshī Devī Prasād in the Archives states that Vikramājīta first locked Mīrā in with a guard, and then, when that failed of the desired effect, made an attempt to poison her, which also failed (cited Padmāvatī p. 151). As the poems attributed to Mīrā refer to a Rānā who locked her in (Poem 42) and tried to poison her (poem 36 etc.), it is presumed that the Rānā in question was Vikramājīta. But the authenticity of the poems referring to the Rānā (Poems 32-42, 50 etc.) is on several counts regarded as doubtful. And in particular, the traditions about the miraculous intervention of the Lord to save Mīrā from various different attempts made by Vikramājīta on her life, even though some of them are referred to in poems that have come down under Mīrā's name, are on the whole not accepted as factual by modern Indian scholarship. On the other hand the notion of an abortive attempt at poisoning is commonly accepted as probable, since it is supported by documentary evidence and by the earliest hagiographical literature. It is supposed by several authorities that Mīrā took refuge with her uncle Vīram Dev in Mertā after the episode of the attempted poisoning, where she remained in company with him and her cousin Jaymal until Vīram Dev was expelled from his own capital by the King of Jodhpur in 1538. Some authorities attribute to this period of Mīrā's life her worship in the Chaturbhuj temple at Mertā, the ruins of which still stand.

Though Munshī Devī Prasād was able to claim some sort of documentary evidence for his account of the birth, marriage and persecution of Mīrā, the rest of her biography can only be guess-work. As the poet Dhruvadās (first half of the Seventeenth Century) mentions that she visited Brindāvan, it is presumed that she became a wandering ascetic and went to Brindāvan on foot after the expulsion of Vīram Dev from Mertā in 1538. The poet Priyādās (first half of the Eighteenth Century), himself a resident of Brindāvan, also claims that Mīrā visited Brindāvan, and adds a colourful anecdote. He says that when in Brindāvan she went to see Jīva Gosvāmī, the famous Teacher of the Chaitanya school. The latter refused to admit her, however, on the ground that she was a woman. Upon this Mīrā is said to have cast Chaitanya's doctrine in his teeth and made the retort : "I used to think that the Lord Krishna was the only man in Brindāvan and that all the rest of the inhabitants were gopīs. Now I've discovered that there's someone else here besides Lord Krishna who thinks of himself as a man." Probably the story is apocryphal. Jīva Gosvāmī would have been living in Brindāvan at the time of the supposed visit. But he would have been a youngish and still obscure Brahmachārī, about thirteen years younger than Mīrā herself, and not the famed Guru of mature years that appears to be implied by the story. (Padmāvatī, p. 158 : P. Chaturvedī, Madhya Kālīna Prem Sādhanā, p. 136)

Whatever be the truth about the visit to and residence in Brindāvan, there is support in Bardic Chronicles and in Mīrā's own poems (e.g. Poem 202) for the belief that she went to Dvārak on the coast of the Kāthiāwār peninsular and lived there a considerable time, worshipping in the "Ranachor" temple. The historian M. M. Gaurīshankar Ojhā (cited Padmāvatī, p. 158) makes Mīrā go direct to Dvārak on leaving Mertā, without any intermediate visit to Brindāvan.

In regard to the date and place of Mīrā's death we are at a loss. Priyādās says that in the course of time evils fell on the city of Chittaur (it was occupied by the Muslims more than once and was finally to be destroyed in 1568) and that the King of Mewār and Mīrā's other family members began to think its decline was due to the persecution of a great devotee. The King therefore sent a deputation of court priests to beg Mīrā to return. Uncertain what to do, Mīrā retired to the temple of Ranachor to pray, and her body melted physically into the image of the deity. In the absence of reliable information about Mīrā's death, the legend provides a fitting image to remember her by. Munshī Devī Prasād dated the event 1546 on the word of the court-minstrel mentioned earlier, which enabled him to pinpoint the King in question as Udaisingh. But the legend has not, on the whole, been accepted by modern Indian scholars as based on fact. Other estimates of the date of Mīrā's death have been given, following stray hints, most of them later than 1546. But there is no settled conclusion.

As already mentioned, Padmāvatī "Shabnam" has reviewed the existing literature on the life of Mīrābāī, and the present sketch is certainly indebted to that part of her labours. She concludes, however, that Munshī Devī Prasād's theory that Mīrā was the grand-daughter of Rāu Dūdā jī and the wife of Bhoja Rāj is altogether untenable. It must be admitted that the "consensus" view (originating from the respected Munshī) is not much more than a guess in regard to all the events in Mīrā's life following the attempted poisoning. But on Mīrā's parentage, her marriage, the persecution instituted be Ratna Singh, and the locking-up and attempted poisoning carried out by Vikramājīta the Munshī was able to cite documents he had found in the Archives of Mewār. Padmāvatī "Shabnam" finds them mutually contradictory and valueless as evidence. (Padmāvatī, p. 45). But in some of the cases she instances, it could perhaps be argued that the documents corroborate one another in substance, while only contradicting one another on points of comparative detail.

However, this is not the place to attempt to assess in detail what can of or cannot be salvaged for the "consensus" view, nor is the present writer equipped for such a task. It will be enough to suggest that it may be analyzable into stronger and weaker parts, if some parts can still be shown to have documentary support. The view to which Padmāvatī "Shabnam" herself inclines is that Mīrā was the daughter (not the grand-daughter) of Dūdā jī and the wife of Rānā Rāymal, who was the father of Rāna Sāngā, and who reigned at Chittaur 1473-1508. There seems to be little positive evidence in favour of this identification. But it obviates the difficulties involved in picturing Mīrā as a widow, when she frequently refers in her poems to her jewelry, and as being persecuted by a young Rānā of 15. More significantly, it brings Mīrā back within the possible time-span of the life of Raidās. This raises the question of the possibility of accepting the four statements in the poems that Raīdās was Mīrā's Guru as the literal truth. It is claimed locally that a strange stone figure opposite the so-called Mīrābāī temple in Chittaur represents the body and the insignia of Raidās. (Chaturvedī, Madhya-Kālīna Prem Sādhanā, p. 137.) But there are difficulties in the way of accepting that Raidās could have been Mīrā's Guru, such as the absence of traditions in the Sant school for connecting Raidās with Mīrā and the presence of traditions that he never left the neighbourhood of Banāras. (Bhuvaneśvara Nātha Miśra, p. 59) And while four of the poems attributed to Mīrā connect her with Raidās, the hagiographical literature does not. Moreover, the reference to Dhannā in Poem 139 of her poems suggests a figure of the fairly distant past whose memory has already become encrusted with miracles, while in one of his own poems Dhannā refers to Raidās as a predecessor. (Macauliffe, p.109) Even if this be regarded as inconclusive on the ground that Poem 139 might be an interpolation, it remains true that there is no documentary evidence in favour of the view that Mīrā was a queen of Rāymal, and what documentary evidence exists is against it, in as much as Padmāvatī herself refers to a list of Rāymal's twelve queens in which Mīrā is not included (Padmāvatī, p.135). And if the poems of Mīrā mentioning a wicked and atheistic Rānā have any historical validity at all, they fit in better with Vikramājīta, who, though only a boy, is known to have been of a vicious temperament, whereas Rāymal is credited with Vaishnava piety and the construction of a temple to Dāmodara at Kumbhalmer fortress in 1498. (Bhuvaneśvara Nātha Miśra, p. 40)

These considerations in partial defence of the "consensus" that Mīrā was married to Bhoja Rāj occurred to the mind and it seemed right to set them down. But as a non-specialist the present writer is in no position to detract from Padmāvatī Shabnam's contribution. If new light on the life of Mīrā and on problems about the authenticity of the poems come down under her name is to come, it can only do so through serious first-hand investigations into the textual sources like hers. If it should eventually turn out that the personal connection between Mīrā and Raidās was established, or even between Mīrā and some member of his school, it would necessitate some rethinking about what poems should be admitted into the standard text of Mīrā's Padāvalī. For instance, some poems written in the technical terminology of the Sant school, excluded by Āchārya Chaturvedī, might have to be included after all. For the moment, however, the question appears to be in the balance. It does not seem that Padmāvatī "Shabnam" has decisively refuted the consensus view.

Mīrā and the Bhakti Movement

Whatever view be taken of the chronology of Mīrā's life, she must have lived in the midst of a great devotional renaissance. If the "consensus" view of her life be approximately correct, Raidās, Kabīr, Vidyāpati, Chaṇḍīdās and Narsī Mehtā were among her immediate forerunners. Sūrdās, Guru Nānak, and the early poets of the schools of Vallabha and Chaitanya were her contemporaries. Tulsīdās, surpassing even Sūrdās as the greatest devotional poèt in Hindī, was probably born towards the latter end of her life-span. In the present essay it is proposed to sketch in the history of the rise of devotion (bhakti) in India and to try to say something about Mīrā's place amidst the various schools.

The word "Bhakti" comes from the root "bhaj" meaning "to share". The basic idea is that God (termed "Bhagavān", also from the root "bhaj") allows His devotees (His "Bhaktas") to share in His own nature and His own Consciousness, if they offer themselves to Him in sincere love. Thus expressed, the term Bhakti implies a distinction between the Lord and His devotee. But amongst the Bhakti schools who offered their devotion to Vishnu, with which the present essay is chiefly concerned, only the "Brahma-Sampradāya" of Shri Madhva (1199-1278) held to the *radical* separateness of the world and the individual souls from God. The main tendency in Hinduism is to stress the unity behind the apparent diversity of the objects of the time-space world, and in general the different cults do just this, in varying ways and with varying degrees of intensity.

The dozen or so "classical" Upanishads commented on by Bhagavatpāda Shankara (circa 700 A.D.) are the highest expression of the "Sanātana Dharma" or "Eternal Wisdom" of orthodox Hinduism. They were probably composed between the eighth and third centuries B.C., the earlier ones being compilations, the later ones more like unitary compositions by a single author. They are regarded as being effective in the spiritual life of a devotee only after their texts have been synthesized into a harmonious whole and interpreted according to a definite tradition (sampradāya), possessing a doctrine that is logically defensible on its own chosen assumptions, the truth of which has been verified by the personal experience of the Teachers who convey it. The Upanishadic teachings thus synthesized are known as the Vedānta, and their exponents as Vedāntins. If we set aside the radically dualistic doctrine of Madhva as exceptional and ignore the Shaiva interpretations of the Vedānta as not relevant to our present enquiry, the chief remaining schools of Vedānta may be divided into two classes, both of which affirm that the real is "non-dual" or "one-without-a-second". To the first class belongs the school of Shankara, maintaining "pure non-duality" (Kevala-advaita). To the second belong the schools of Rāmānuja, Nimbārka, Vallabha and Chaitanya. This second group of Āchāryas ranges in date from the eleventh to the sixteenth century. Like the school of Shankara, its members also maintain the "non-duality" of the real; but unlike Shankara they credit it in various ways with real internal distinctions.

For Shankara, the world and its distinctions are illusory, as is the distinction between the individual soul and the supreme non-dual Self in which, as pure undifferentiated Consciousness, the whole illusion rests. For him, devotion to God conceived in limited or personal form is a most wholesome and purifying practice. But it is only a preliminary. Final liberation from evil only comes through the *knowledge* that one is identical with the supreme Self that supports all as infinite, undifferentiated Consciousness. This knowledge or awakening comes primarily from hearing the supreme Upanishadic texts from a competent Teacher who himself has direct intuitional awareness of the truth of their content. Even then, the texts can normally only do their work after the student has prepared himself to understand them by a disciplined life, (yama and niyama), and by reflection (manana) and prolonged meditation on the Upanishadic texts under the guidance of the Guru.

In the other Vedānta schools mentioned, it is generally speaking knowledge that is the preliminary and devotion the crowning part of the discipline. They regard the world and its objects and also the multiplicity of souls as distinct emanations from the Lord. But the Lord is present in all, He inhabits His creation, and He animates all living beings with a "ray" of His consciousness and is, in a specially intimate sense, "present in their hearts". The goal of the spiritual life is for the individual to disentangle himself from attachment to and identification with the body and to become aware that in his essential nature he is homogeneous with the supreme Spirit (puruṣottama), a ray of the latter and able to enjoy a love-relation with Him, conceived in personal form. The Lord might rescue such a soul from the ocean of transmigratory life and transport him to His heaven on the death of the physical body, there for him to remain in perpetual adoration and felicity.

The Vedānta, however, is not based exclusively on the Upanishads. It has three starting-points (prasthāna) in the classical Upanishads, the Brahma Sūtras and the Bhagavad Gītā. The Brahma Sūtras are the authoritative digest of the Upanishads, and the Āchāryas developed their systems by writing commentaries on them, each interpreting their terse formulae according to his own peculiar logic. The collection of Sūtras as we have them probably grew into existence gradually during (and before) the early centuries of the Christian era. They refer to the Bhagavad Gītā as an authoritative text, the composition of the latter being often dated vaguely to about 200 B.C., since it quotes the later classical Upanishads, some of which appear to have been composed after Buddhism had spread.

The Vedānta is really a synthesis between the Vedic religion, developed by the Aryan invaders, and other forms of Indian worship with roots probably stretching back before Aryan times. (Cp. De, pp. 162-176). The later Upanishadic period saw a challenge to the old Vedic religion and to the authority of the Brahmins who preserved it. On the one hand, teachers like Gautama Buddha and Mahāvīra were attacking its sacrificial ritual as cruel and its caste system as unhumanitarian, and were giving ethical and spiritual instructions of a high order in the vernacular. On the other hand the old Vedic religion was itself falling into decay. What had begun as outdoor worship of the personified forces of nature later soared to the heights of true mysticism when the sages "pondered in their hearts, searching for the link between non-being and being". But it finally degenerated into a soulless formalism, in which the meticulous performance of the complicated ritual counted ever for more and more and the deity for less and less. The Upanishads, it is true, contained texts unfolding the highest wisdom attainable by man. But in the form in which they were preserved, these texts were addressed only to those members of the higher castes who had leisure in youth to learn the Vedic texts by heart, and to that small percentage of these which was willing to abandon household life and take to the forests.

Oversimplifying somewhat, we may say that the response of Brahminical orthodoxy to the challenge of the "heretical" religions was to allow the old Vedic religion to fall into comparative relapse and to adopt and refashion themes of popular worship. We see various stages of this process registered in the Epics (Mahābhārata including the Gītā and the Rāmāyaṇa), in the earlier Purāṇas, and later in the Tantras. Included in it was the adoption of the ancient Bhāgavata religion, which gradually assumed a revised form in which Bhagavān was identified with Vāsudeva and Krishna, and both with the old Vedic deity Vishnu.

Meister Eckhart has said that it is the birth of Christ in the heart of the devotee *now* that matters, not so much His birth in Bethlehem many years ago. The "historical Krishna" revealed (or rather not revealed) by modern scholarship is no more the Krishna who revealed Himself in the hearts of the saints of mediaeval India than the "historical Jesus" of modern Biblical scholarship is the figure that lit the hearts of St. Francis and St. Bonaventura. The historical Krishna is in fact even more elusive than the historical Jesus. But Āchārya Chaturvedī thinks we have just about enough evidence to think of him as a great warrior and Teacher, a Kshatria of the Yādava tribe, who received spiritual instruction at the hands of Ghora Āngirasa (Chāndogya Upanishad III. vii. 6), who slew King Kansa at Mathurā, who supported the Pāṇḍavas in the Mahābhārata war, and who was eventually deified by the later generations of those who followed his teaching. (Chaturvedī, Vaishnava Dharma, p. 32) Those who take this view commonly maintain that the Bhagavad Gītā preserves the essence of Krishna's teaching. Admittedly its teachings do not agree very well with what is known of those of Ghora Āngirasa. (De, p. 32 ff.) But at any rate it was *taken* by the Bhaktas of mediaeval India as the personal word of Krishna. And it marks an important phase in the restatement of the Upanishadic wisdom in a more popular form and with increased stress on the element of devotion.

Indeed, the Gītā can be viewed partly as an attempt to popularize the Upanishadic teachings and bring them to a wider circle. The author tries to preserve all that was great and profound in the earlier teaching and at the same time to make it available to all men of good will, living and working in the world. The Upanishadic doctrine that liberation arises through attaining an intuitive knowledge of one's identity with the world-ground (brahma-nirvāṇa) is allowed to stand. But the peculiar path of renunciation of worldly life and solitary meditation on abstract principles which leads to it is declared "hard". The prime purpose of the Gītā is to teach an easier path to liberation. This easier path has two phases. The first consists in self-purification through disinterested action (karma-yoga). The second consists in devotion to the Absolute conceived in personal form (bhakti-yoga). The devotion called for in the Gītā seems to be something a great deal stronger than the mere meditation on the Absolute associated with this or that finite form enjoined in the sections of the Upanishads concerned with worship (upāsanā-kāṇḍa). It means living in the faith and conviction that one participates in the nature of God, in such a way that one concentrates all one's powers on God as the great whole of which one is a severed fragment, desiring above all to be re-united with the whole. The devotee understands that he cannot know God in His true form. But He conceives Him under forms that inspire deep awe and reverence, and he expresses his love for Him in service of His creatures. The Gītā does not specify whether the sincere devotee is dissolved in God at death or whether he retains his individuality. Though it speaks of the soul as a "ray" of God, it does not mention the delights of a sojourn in Vishnu's heaven. So Shankara's view that complete dissolution is meant is at least defensible. It is a remarkable point that Mīrā looks forward to complete dissolution in God at death (Poem 46, last 2 lines), whereas the great Vaishnava Teachers of the Middle Ages, such as Rāmānuja, Madhva, Nimbārka, Vallabha and Chaitanya speak, in general, of the released soul retaining its individuality after death and enjoying felicity in one form or another in the adoration of the Lord.

The texts conveying Bhakti we have considered so far were all composed in Sanskrit and therefore, in general, immediately available only to those of the top three castes who had the leisure to learn that beautiful but complicated language. Nevertheless, it was beginning to be affirmed more frequently that all men had access to salvation through the texts of the Epics and Purāṇas, even if the hearing of the Veda and Upanishads was confined to the "twice-born", the three higher castes. These castes did in fact manage to preserve their position and dominance and keep the tradition of memorizing the Vedic and Upanishadic texts alive. But in the face of the criticism of Materialists, Buddhists and Jainas and of the apathy of many of their own members, who found little appeal either in cold Vedic ritualism or in abstruse Upanishadic speculation, adaptations had to be made. The Brahmins absorbed into their own system many originally independent conceptions of the deity by identifying them with the deity Vishnu from their own pantheon. From his dignified but comparatively subordinate role as sun-deity in the Rig Veda, Vishnu was elevated to the state of supreme Spirit and identified with Bhagavān, Vāsudeva, Krishna, Nārāyaṇa and other less widely known divine figures, so that the cults and beliefs associated with these deities were mingled together and applied to Him. Similarly, the worship of the comparatively minor Rig Vedic deity Rudra was altered and expanded to incorporate new myths and new practices under the name of Shaivism or Shiva-worship. Borrowing and adaptation from the practices and beliefs originally belonging to the non-Aryan indigenous population played a large part in all this process. Indeed, the shock of the contact between the Aryan invaders and the pre-Aryan inhabitants had already been a factor in producing the creative tension that led to the lofty teaching of the classical Upanishads, not to speak of the various phases of the Buddhist and Jaina religions. But with the advent of Vaishnavism and Shaivism, the non-Aryan element came even more to the fore. By the time of the Tāntrika and Shākta movements, beginning in the latter half of the first millennium A.D., when the sectarian texts were addressing themselves to men and women of all castes and openly declaring that they had supplanted the Veda as the vehicle of salvation for men in the Iron Age (Kali Yuga), it was no longer a question of the old Aryan religion absorbing non-Aryan elements but rather of its being itself absorbed by that age-old "Mother India", already evident in the ancient Mahenjo Daro civilization.

As the period of the Vedic revelation proper (Shruti) gave way to that of the derivative literature (Smriti), the latter being at its height between 200 B.C. and 500 A.D., a whole new mythology was developed in the Law Books (Dharma Shāstra, the Smriti *par excellence*), the Epics and the earlier Purāṇas. After a comparatively weak challenge from the old Vedic gods Brahmā, Agni and Sūrya, the two Vedic deities Shiva (formerly Rudra) and Vishnu came to dominate. Their cult was emancipated from its setting in the old Vedic texts, and drew fresh nourishment and new vigour from association with popular local cults. It was in considerable part to this process that Vishnu owed His "Thousand Names". The new religion had an exterior form consisting of image-worship (pūjā) in temples, quite unknown in the Vedic texts; and it had an interior or mental form, in which the deity was approached through newly devised methods of meditation as resident within the body of the worshipper. Repetition with a rosary of short formulae embodying the name of the deity worshipped (mantra-japa) is to be accounted among the new techniques. The earliest references connect it with the worship of Shiva, but the formula "Om namo Vāsudevāya" is already found referred to Vishnu in the fifth century literature, which is a sign that the actual practice of repeating it must have begun considerably earlier. The other ancient deities of the Vedic pantheon lost status in comparison to Shiva and Vishnu, as is well symbolized in the early chapters of the Tenth Book of the Bhāgavata Purāṇa, where the child Krishna humiliates Brahmā and Indra. Mīrā refers to the humiliation of Indra in the opening poem of the Padāvalī.

The Vishnu of the Mahābhārata and early Purāṇas is included

in Mīrā's conception of the Lord (Prabhu), but is not the only or the foremost element. According to the earlier conception He "manifested" (prādurbhāva) again and again in different forms to save His devotees from the attacks of the evil forces and to preserve the spiritual law when it was in danger of falling into neglect. According to a rather later conception Vishnu undertook "descents" (avatāra) not only to relieve the immediate sufferings of His devotees and to kill demons plaguin the earth but also to leave behind amongst His devotees a memory of His deeds (līlā), meditation on which would serve to purify the whole world of its sins. (cp. Adhyātma Rāmāyaṇa, opening verse, Kīrtim pāpa-haraṁ vidhāya jagatām)

During the course of the first millennium A.D. a new form of the worship of Krishna gradually developed, not found in the older texts and mysterious in origin. Krishna the warrior and counsellor began to fall more and more into the background, and gradually the chief emphasis came to be placed on worship of Krishna as a boy of wondrous beauty, growing up from childhood to adolescence in the villages of cowherds on the banks of the Jumna a few miles upstream from Mathurā. The child Krishna is hardly known to the Mahābhārata, but His deeds are recorded in the Vishnu Purāṇa and Harivansha (fifth century A.D.). Parallel with this development, though not intimately connected with it, temple-worship was developed both in Vaishnava and Shaiva circles. Shankara Bhagavatpāda, who effected the earliest surviving synthesis between the doctrines of the Veda, the Epic and the Purāṇas, speaks with marked sympathy of the devotional practices of the worshippers of Vishnu, even though he criticizes their theory of "Vyūhas" in so far as he found it unreconcilable with Upanishadic non-dualism. (Brahma Sūtra Commentary II.ii.42) He enumerates them as visiting the temple (abhigamana); concentrating on Vāsudeva (Krishna) in thought, word and deed; offering of articles before the image; active worship of the image in the form of bathing it, anointing it and decorating it with flowers; repetition of the eight-syllabled mantram (Om namo Nārāyaṇāya); and meditative practices (yoga-dhyāna). (cp. H. P. Dvivedī, Madhya-kālīna Dharma Sādhanā, p. 124)

During this time, if not before it, the creative impulse in devotion to Krishna passed to South India. The twelve devotees of Tamil Nād known as the Ālvārs, who apparently lived in second half of the first millennium A.D., composed devotional hymns in the vernacular, celebrating Vishnu both in His form as the child Krishna and also according to the earlier traditional conceptions. They paid little attention to caste-distinctions and included in their number a king, a woman and several outcastes. The work of the Ālvārs was valued and preserved by the "Āchāryas" of the Śrī Sampradāya, high-caste representatives of the Vedānta tradition, mostly monks, but more intimately associated with the temple-worship of lay folk than Shankara had been. They wrote commentaries in Sanskrit and produced a new synthesis of the Vedānta (Upanishads) and the derivative literature (Epics, Gītā and Purāṇas). They claimed to go back behind Shankara to earlier commentators on the Brhama Sūtras whose work is now lost. But in fact the old Upanishadic teachings were partly modified in the light of texts from the Gītā, Mahābhārata and Vishnu Purāṇa so as to accommodate devotion to the Lord conceived in personal form as the supreme discipline. The greatest figure in this movement was Rāmānuja (second half of the eleventh century). Though a representative of orthodox Brahmanism, he partly relaxed the tradition according to which only the three higher castes had access to the Vedāntic truth.

Rāmānuja has been thought of as the link between Bhakti as a popular movement in the South and Bhakti as a popular movement in the North. For on the one hand he called the Tamil works of the "outcaste" Śaṭhakopa Āchārya the "Veda of the Vaishnavas" and helped to preside over their preservation. And on the other hand it is said to have been an Āchārya of his line residing in Banāras, Rāghavānanda, who initiated Rāmānanda, who is in turn said to have been the father of the Sant tradition of Northern India, of whom more must be said below. Perhaps too much should not be made of this connection. For none of the Sants actually mention Rāmānanda as their Guru. (Chaturvedī, Sant Paramparā p. 224f.) And Rāmānanda is in any case said to have broken with Rāghavānanda because the latter still adhered too much to caste distinctions. Perhaps

Rāmānanda's service to the Bhakti movement was to create the climate in which the Sants could give out their message. He is said to have inspired people to carry the message that all who worshipped Hari formed one great brotherhood quite independent of caste and to have set the example of instructing unlettered folk in the vernacular about remembrance of the Name of God.

But South India produced one other phenomenon in the latter half of the first millennium A.D. that was an even more potent aid to the development of Krishna Bhakti than the Śrī Sampradāya of Rāmānuja, and that was the composition of the Bhāgavata Purāṇa (circa 800 A.D.). This magnificent work appears to have remained for several centuries after its composition in comparative obscurity. Rāmānuja, for instance, does not mention it. But Nimbārka, Vallabha and Chaitanya regarded it as of at least equal authority with the Veda. It gives in fact what might be called the standard or classical account both of the sports of Krishna as child and adolescent and of the devotional tenets of the Vaishnava faith.

Mīrā touches so lightly on the scenes of Krishna's childhood depicted in the Bhāgavata that it hardly seems necessary to give any connected summary of the narrative here. The reader will find in Mīrā's Padāvalī brief references to the childish sports of the Lord in the Braj, which must derive directly or indirectly from the Bhāgavata. Such are the expulsion of the snake Kāliya from Braj, (Poem 1 and 168) the stealing of the clothes of the cowherd-maidens when they were bathing (applied by Mīrā to herself, conceived as a Gopī), (Poem 169) the morning ritual of setting off to pasture the cows, (165) and holding the Govardhana Mountain aloft to protect the inhabitants of Braj from the fury of Indra. (1) In general, however, Mīrā does not undertake to re-depict the sports of the Lord objectively. (Cp. Bhuvaneshvara Nātha Mishra, p. 196) Rather, she records episodes in her own private love-relationship with the Lord. Like the Ālvār poetess Godā, she believed herself to have been a Gopī in a former birth.

In one or two poems Mīrā refers to the Gopī (cowherd-maiden) Rādhā. Building upon hints in the Bhāgavata and other Vaishnava literature (and drawing also on local folkloric traditions) great poets of the order of Jai Dev and Chaṇḍīdās in Bengal and Vidyāpati in Darbhangā had developed the theme of a personal love-affair between Krishna and one of the Gopīs, Rādhā. H.P. Dvivedī has drawn attention to the idealism latent in the character of Rādhā as depicted by these poets. (Madhya-Kālīna Dharma Sādhanā, p. 159, 183, 194). But even allowing for such elements and for the fact that some of this poetry may be intended as an illustration of how ordinary human sex-love can be transfigured and raised to the plane of the love of God according to the tenets of the Vaishnava Sahajiyā sect, (Chaturvedī, Prem Sādhanā p. 85 f.) it does seem to imply a markedly different conception of devotion from that of Mīrā. So far as the writer's very limited acquaintance with it goes, it seems to be extraordinarily brilliant poetry composed by connoisseurs for connoisseurs. Jai Dev addresses his "Padāvalī" (i.e. the Gīta-Govinda) to the mind which has a taste for remembrance of Hari *and* an enthusiasm for the fine arts (vilāsa-kaḷā). And it is a commonly held view that whereas the erotic element in the Bhāgavata Purāṇa, though present, is a mere phase of the devotional element, in parts of the poetry now under discussion the erotic element tends to get the upper hand. Vrajeshvara Varmā claims (in Dhīrendra Varmā, p. 353) that Vidyāpati's Padāvalī is pure secular love poetry, and that about half the poems do not concern Rādhā and Krishna at all.

In any case there is nothing highly-wrought about Mīrā's style, and no erotic element in her poetry whatever. (Bhuvaneshvara Nātha Mishra, p. 195) Mastery of the elements of versification and music are taken for granted. But Mīrā was primarily a devotee, and if she was a poetess or a musician or anything else whatever, that was secondary (Chaturvedī, Madhya-kālīna Prem Sādhanā, p. 130) She borrows many of the traditional *clichés* of Indian love-poetry that are also found in Vidyāpati and Chaṇḍīdās. But with her they are instruments used to express a deep and *personally felt* emotion. She may use the marriage-bed as a symbol of mystical union with God, in the manner of the Sant poets, or as a symbol of the devotee's readiness to give the Lord all that is in his power. But in Mīrā's poetry there is no tendency to luxuriate in devotional feelings tinged with eroticism. So she is not faced with the danger that besets the poet who evokes images of the Lord in the context of burning sexual passion, the danger of making the deity *less* than a person, of reducing Him to a kind of object, a source of exquisite emotions that is available to the devotee and, so to speak, "stands at his disposal". (Hacker, p. 51) Neither is Mīrā in any way influenced by the tendency found in some of the later Purāṇas to elevate Rādhā into the Cosmic Power of the Lord or even to worship her in her own right as the Divine Mother. Her Rādhā is simply an especially charming fellow-devotee, who grieves when her Lord is "absent" and does all she can to please Him when He is present, as a good devotee should.

The present writer cannot discuss in any detail the resemblances and differences between Mīrā and the greatest of her contemporaries amongst Krishna-poets, Sūr Dās, for lack of a proper first-hand acquaintance with the sources. Clearly she was not Sūr Dās's equal technically as a poet. In spirit they seem to stand close. Both were true devotees of the Lord. Sūr painted scenes and incidents from the life of Krishna as child and youth. Mīrā expressed a more personal associationship with the Lord. One might have expected that, as a pupil of Vallabha, Sūr would have looked forward to an eternity in Krishna's heaven (Go-loka) after death, whereas Mīrā begged for dissolution in the Lord. But it appears that the difference on this score was not great. Verses occur in Sūr's poetry in which he asks to be transported to Vaikuṇṭha (Go-loka) and also others where he asks for "dissolution" (nirvāṇa). But these requests pale in number and significance before his chief request, which was "Grant me devotion." (Brajveshvara Varmā p. 209) Both he and Mīrā were concerned with the here and now rather than with the hereafter. And this is the true attitude of the mystic.

qasr firdaus bapādāsh 'amal mībakshand
mā kah rindīm o gadā dair mughān mārā bas

Conventional piety brings its reward,
A mansion in Paradise;
But for a ragamuffin sinner like me,
A seat in the tavern is enough.

(*Hāfiz*)

It has often been remarked that the occasional references to Mīrā in the later devotional literature of Vallabha's school suggest that she was regarded as an outsider, an irregular devotee who did not belong to any recognized tradition (sampradāya). In Āchārya Chaturvedī's revised (fifteenth) edition of the Poems there is only one reference to a Guru, (Poem 111) and the particular technical term used (Sat-Guru) suggests association with the Sant school. Shrī Chaturvedī has expressed doubts about the authenticity of this reference, and even if it should prove authentic it need not necessarily point to a single Guru of the Sant school. The Sants speak so often of the Sat-Guru and so seldom of any particular Guru that modern scholars have come to wonder whether the term may not be applicable to *any* Guru from association (Satsang) with whom one has learned spiritually valuable lessons. Often the Sat-Guru is the inner "voice" (jñāna, viveka, śabda) heard by the poet in the interior depths of his own soul. (Chaturvedī, Sant-Paramparā p. 162 f. : Vaudeville, p. 116 f., p. 137) In Poem 139 of Mīrā's Padāvalī, which, again, may or may not be authentic, there are references to miraculous interventions by the Lord to save His devotees, who include the Sants Kabīr, Nāma Deva and Dhannā. But even if it should turn out that the lines or poems referring directly to a Sat-Guru or to the Sants by name have to be rejected, there are still plenty of lines in the Poems that echo the Sants' teaching.

It is difficult to characterize the Teachers of the Sant school briefly, and they each had their own marked individuality. They were unlettered Teachers of low caste, who had been giving out ethical and spiritual instruction on the plains of Northern India for some generations before Mīrā's birth. The style of their songs and many of the technical terms they used were inherited from earlier Teachers of Northern India called Siddhas and Nāthas. The Siddhas in their turn inherited much from the Buddhist Tāntrika Teachers who had survived in Bengal, Assam and Tibet when the Muslims had overrun most of the Ganges plain.

The basic idea behind the Tāntrika teaching and practice here in question is that the whole cosmos is shot through with divine powers. These powers are also present in the body of the adept and can be awakened by suitable ritual or physiological practices. In some of the poems attributed to him, the Sant Kabīr speaks language which seems to point to experiences gained through arousing the "kuṇḍalinī" through the various yogic "chakras" till it reaches the "thousand-petalled lotus" in the top of the head. And there seem to be references to yogic practices of this kind in poems that are linked with Mīrā's name but which are not allowed admittance into Āchārya Chaturvedī's collection in its present form. Equally, there are poems attributed to each author denouncing such practices, especially if not accompained by the one practice, that really matters, continuous remembrance of the holy Name. (Cp. Vaudeville, p. 143)

Even in the present (fifteenth) edition of Shrī Chaturvedī's version of Mīrā's Padāvalī, however, which excludes some well-known poems which refer to Raidās as a personal Guru and others which refer to yogic chakras, there remain plenty of echoes of Sant teaching, which may be attributed to what she heard when mingling with the Sādhus. But her resort to temples for dancing and singing (Poem 31 etc.) and her practice of Pūjā of images (Poem 145) set her somewhat apart from the classical Sant tradition. One can hardly imagine Kabīr or Raīdās dancing or performing Pūjā in a temple. Mīrā uses the word "Rāma" to mean God in general, which is a typical practice of the Sants. But whereas they tended to speak of their God either as "featureless" (nirguṇa) or as "not even featureless" (i.e. totally indescribable), and seem to have used the word "Rāma" mainly because it was in vogue, Mīrā definitely connects the name Rāma with the visible image of her beloved Shyāma (Shrī Krishna). (See Poem 16) In the opening line of Poem 187 she uses the word Rāma to refer to Krishna as He greets His former play-fellow Sudāmā. It must be remembered that Kabīr and the Sants of his time generally were more preoccupied than Mīrā was with reconciling Hindu-Muslim differences. They therefore attacked many things which they considered tended to divide but which Mīrā held dear, such as worship of images, observance of special fasts (Cp. Poem 145) and, above all, the doctrine that Vishnu "descended" to earth. This last was central to Mīrā's faith, as she believed herself to have been with Krishna in a previous life.

Possibly it would be right to say that Mīrā's deepest spiritual affinities lie not with the brilliant and sophisticated court-poets of the North East (Jai Dev etc.), nor with the brilliant temple-poets of Braj (school of Vallabha) nor with the "Nirguṇa-Vāda" Sants of Uttara Pradesh, Rājasthān and the Punjāb, but rather with the Krishna-devotees of Mahārāshtra and Gujarāt. It cannot be said that the mysticism of the saints of Mahārāshtra recalls the intimately personal relationship of Mīrā with her "Giridhara Nāgara". But they are similar to Mīrā in their acceptance of temple-worship and devotion to Krishna personally conceived, along with emphasis on the remembrance of the Name and the view that devotion has a supreme phase that eventually culminates in dissolution in the deity.

For example, Jñāneshvara (1271-1293) composed in old Marāthī a famous verse commentary on the Gītā which has more than once been translated into English. One of the remarkable points about this work is that, though its predominant tone is devotional, some passages (as in the Shrīmad Bhāgavata) strike the note of Shankara's pure non-dualism. (Cp. Gonda, p. 218 f.) Thus in the exordium to the Sixteenth Chapter paying honour to his Guru Nivrittinātha as the sun of knowledge, he says: "When the sun reaches the zenith of Self-knowledge and shines down 'in the noon-tide of Realization of the Absolute (brahma-bhāva)', its shadow, the false self of illusion (the individual ego of ordinary unregenerate experience), retires and becomes hidden beneath it, and then the 'night of Māyā' no longer exists, the world disappears and the sleep of wrong knowledge no longer has any foundation." Mīrā does not hark back to the terminology of the Upanishads in this way. But she affirms the fundamental identity of the individual soul with the Lord, and begs to be dissolved in Him. "Thou and I are one, like the sun and its heat" (Poem 114) and "Let my light dissolve in Your light before You depart."(46)

With the name of Jñāneshvara is linked that of Nām Dev, formerly taken to have been his contemporary, but now considered later by a century. He is probably to be identified with the poet of the same name who composed works in Hindī which are included in the Guru Granth Sāhib. (Chaturvedī, Sant-Paramparā p. 105) Nām Dev also speaks language that comes close to the pure non-dualism of Shankara. The devotee (jana) and God (Ṭhākur) become one, like water poured into water. (Compare, once again, the last lines of Mīrā's Poem 46) The deity, the temple, the act of worship are all one, as waves and bubbles are only water. If one dances and sings before an image, it is the image itself that is dancing and singing. Nām Dev regarded the remembrance of the holy Name of God as superior to ritual, charity or bathing in holy places. He supports this claim with examples derived from the Purāṇas. It is clear from her Padāvalī that Mīrā did not think otherwise. Remembrance of the Name is the constant inner practice on the part of the adept, and is not confined to the repetition of the Name with a rosary. It was so with the Teachers of the Nātha school. (Vaudeville, p.140) It was so with Nām Dev. And it is still so with India's holy men of the present century. When Swāmī Rāma Tīrtha tripped and nearly stumbled over, he said "For a moment, Rāma forgot Rāma."

Remembrance of the Name, then, is a fundamental item in Mīrā's spritual sādhanā, more fundamental than the exterior discipline of worshipping the deity in the temple, more fundamental than the singing and dancing associated with the "Mīrā" of popular conception. But few can absorb themselves directly in the Absolute in its true nature as featureless (nirguṇa). Though the true nature of the Lord is to be without limitation or form (Mīrā's "Hari avināsī"), remembrance of the Name is usually associated with a mental image. Though the devotee knows that any conception of the deity he may form is inadequate, he nevertheless endows Him with visible form by "applying to his eyes the antimony of love." (Brahma-Sanhitā, quoted H. P. Dvivedī, Dharma Sādhanā p. 13) As the devout Christian imagines himself in the presence of Christ, so the Bhakta imagines himself in the presence of Krishna, Rāma or Hanumān. The Ālvār Godā saw the South Indian village in which she lived as Brindāvan, the other village-girls, her companions, as Gopīs, the villiage temple as the house of the foster-father of Krishna, Nanda, and the image it contained as Krishna Himself.

Similarly the Gujarātī saint Narsī Mehtā, who was probably born about eighty years before Mīrā and with whose works she may well have been familiar, says: "I went to Dvāraka with

Shiv Himself and held aloft a burning torch while Krishna and Rādhā danced. I was so lost in the unparalleled sight that my hand was burnt by the torch before I was even aware of it." And again : "I took the hand of that Lover of the Gopīs in loving converse... I forgot all else. Even my manhood left me. I began to sing and dance like a woman. My body seemed to change and I became one of the Gopīs. I acted as a go-between like a woman, and began to lecture Rādhā for being too proud... At such times I experienced moments of incomparable sweetness and joy. He who was sitting, singing with Rādhā was also at that very time seated in my own heart." (Chaturvedī, Madhur-opāsanā p. 40 f., quoting from K.M. Munshī, Gujarāt and its Literature, pp. 190-1) If God is symbolized in human form as Krishna, then the devotee can approach God most intimately by imagining himself as a Gopī or as Rādhā. Naturally this can be done with greatest intensity by a woman-devotee like Mīrā, already equipped by nature with a woman's heart. (Chaturvedī, *op. cit.* p. 74, f.)

There is, however, a further point to note about Mīrā's love-relationship with the Lord. Generally speaking, devotee-poets of Krishna, whether they see themselves in a love-relation with the Lord like Mīrā or merely depict His love-relationships with the Gopīs or Rādhā, were apt to conceive the relation as an illicit one. The Gopīs are considered model devotees because, when they heard the sound of Krishna's flute at night they abandoned their husbands and homes and sped at once to answer the call. They preferred the tension of an illicit relationship that defied convention to the torpor of conformity with worldly values. But Mīrā had no need to imagine an illicit relationship to demonstrate how a devotee defies worldly convention, as she had already publicly defied worldly convention by the intensity of her religious life and by her determination to frequent the company of holy men at all costs. In fact Mīrā speaks very little of the Gopīs. (Cp. Bhuvaneshvara Nātha Mishra, p. 196) Her poetry expresses her personal love-relationship with the Lord, which is predominantly conceived as that of an utterly dedicated Hindu wife.

Mīrā resembled Narsī Mehtā and her contemporary Chaitanya in expressing vehement emotion by dancing and singing.

(Chaturvedī, Sant-Paramparā p. 91) We have seen that it is when viewed in this light that she seems furthest removed from Sants like Kabīr and Raidās. Yet in other ways she resembles them. Raidās re-affirmed from outside the ranks of orthodox caste Hinduism the old principle of Shankara's Advaita that no devotional practices are meaningful unless they lead to *knowledge* of the final truth in the end. "What are dancing and singing, austerities and clasping of the feet, if the Truth be not known?" (kahā bhayo nāce aru gāye/kahā bhayo tapa kīnheṃ//kahā bhayo je caraṇa pakāre/jauṃlauṃ tattva na cīnheṃ? Viyogī Hari, p. 190) He saw this knowledge as the melting of difference into non-difference(tab bheda abheda samāvaigā, *ibid.*) And this insight into the absence of difference is attained through the grace of the Guru and remembrance of the Name. Raidās was united with the Lord "like borax with gold", and this was also Mīrā's ideal, as we have seen.

In this refusal to remain content with worship of the Lord conceived in manifest form (saguṇa), in this demand to realize her final *identity* with the Lord, Mīrā stands apart from the great Vedāntic schools of Bhakti founded by Rāmānuja, Madhva, Nimbārka, Vallabha and Chaitanya. On the other hand her preoccupation with temple worship in its more emotional forms sets her apart from the typical low-caste Sants of Northern India, who nevertheless agree with her that the goal of the spiritual life is the transcendence of all finitude. (Cp. Padmāvatī, p. 185f.) It is not that she speaks of Krishna as "beyond form" (nirguṇa), at least in the poems here presented of the Padāvalī. And yet there is some truth in the striking remark of P.D. Baṛathvāl that she was "a Gopī whose Krishna was the Absolute." No doubt she is unclassifiable, as has often been said. But in her refusal to draw a line between worship of God face to face and complete dissolution in the deity she seems to stand closer to the school of Jñāneshvara than to any other. (Cp. Chaturvedī, Madhuropāsanā p. 82) Two texts of Jñāneshvara express in philosophical form the mystery of the combination of devotion to God with a sense of one's final identity with God which we encounter in the poetry of Mīrā. He says: "If you can hew out of the rock a cave which contains a temple, the image of God and the figures of a concourse of worshippers, why cannot you combine non-dualism with devotion?" And again: "The fact that intuition of non-duality can be combined with devotion is a matter of immediate experience. It can never be explained in words." (Quoted Chaturvedī, Vaishnava Dharma p. 120)

Mīrā's Poems

Mīrā's poetical works are conventionally referred to as her "Padāvalī". The word Padāvalī means a series of padas. The term pada was used by the popular preachers of the Siddha and Nātha schools who preceded Kabīr. The pada in its more mature form was a short song conveying instruction on the spiritual life, usually rhyming and composed in simple rhythms, adaptable for singing. The melody (rāg) to which they should be sung is specified, and they would usually have a Dhruvak or refrain for their opening or second line. The author's name is incorporated in the last line as a kind of signature.

The great Sanskrit poet Jai Dev refers to his Gīta Govinda as a Padāvalī in the proem. Here the word "āvalī" or series has a special significance, as the work is conceived as suitable for dramatic production. But this is not the case with the Padāvalīs of the popular religious poets of mediaeval India. They did not write their poems, but just composed and sang them from time to time. In some cases, for example in the case of Kabīr, Guru Nānak, Sūr and Dādu, attempts were made to reduce their work to writing fairly soon after their death. But this was not so in the case of Mīrā. Her songs simply survived in the mouths of itinerant singers who learned them, sang them, sometimes altered them and added to them, and passed them on.

Various attempts have been made from the latter part of the last century on to collect and print Mīrā's poems and some manuscript collections as well as printed editions exist. A modern edition of Mīrā's poems cannot be anything more than a miscellaneous collection of songs that have come down under her name, pruned of extraneous material by the editor so far as he is able and arranged in whatever order seemed to him good. Āchārya Chaturvedī's edition of the Padāvalī first appeared well over thirty years ago, but on the occasion of the fifteenth edition in 1973 he subjected the text to considerable revision, partly in the light of material published in the intervening years and partly in the light of manuscript material made available to him by friends.

Shrī Chaturvedī's 1973 edition comprehends 202 songs, plus eighteen songs which include the use of the terminology of the Sant school, considered by him to be doubtful and placed in an Appendix. No attempt to translate this latter group has been made here. He also considers the songs containing conversations between Mīrā and her relatives inauthentic. He accepts the poems in which Mīrā threatens to become a "Jogin" or pictures Krishna as a Jogī, while remarking that they should not be made a ground for supposing that Mīrā was an initiate of or subscribed to tenets of the Jogīs of the Nāth school. Shrī Chaturvedī's editition does not aim to be all-inclusive. Svāmī Ānanda Svarūp's "Mīrā Sudhāsindhu" contains 1312 songs and Padmāvatī "Shabnam's" "Brihad Pada Sangraha" 590. The last-named, in her "Mīrān Vyaktitva aur Krititva" (1973), has collected more material and suggested new methods of classification of the songs and comparison of the different versions. Eventually a new picture of the Padāvalī may emerge, but for the present the edition of such an experienced hand as Shrī Chaturvedī may be allowed to constitute a kind of standard version.

Everyone agrees that Mīrā's songs have been much tailored and altered by the singers who sang them. They are mostly in Rājasthānī or Braj Bhāshā, but also contain material in Gujarātī, Panjābī or even Eastern Hindī. (Chaturvedī, Padāvalī p. 58) On the whole, the linguistic forms that have come down in the Padāvalī seem to correspond with geographical data of Mīrā's life as reconstructed by modern scholarship. Her childhood and youth in Rājasthān would account for the Rājasthānī base. Her travels to Braj and Dvārak and her mingling with holy men would account for the sprinkling of other dialects. (Chaturvedī, *ibid.*)

Mīrā's songs, being eminently popular and "singable" in style were evidently much sung in different places, and the versions of them which have come down to us owe part of their linguistic colouring to the local dialects of the singers who have sung them. In many cases, what have come down to us as different songs are really only different versions of one song made at different times by different singers. (Padmāvatī, p. 82) The more popular the song, the more numerous the alternative versions are apt to be. Where there are several alternative versions of one song, the extra verses in the longer versions are inclined to be suspect, especially if any element of "modernity" is betrayed by their linguistic forms. No doubt this helps to account for the absence of familiar lines in several of the poems as printed in Chaturvedī's text. (See e.g. Poems 12, 18, 154, 193)

The spiritual teaching in Mīrā's Padāvalī, which is what most interests the person who reads her songs in English, may be summarized as follows, drawing largely on Āchārya Chaturvedī's work. Mīrā's experiences of death and bereavement in a Rājpūt family taught her the flimsiness of all worldly supports. Life is short. The body will soon mingle with the dust. (Poem 156) Whatever mode of human life be adopted, it will be like the sporting of sparrows that will end at nightfall. (195) Committing suicide at a holy place or the formal adoption of the life of a monk will not help, as without the intervention of the Lord one remains caught in the net of rebirth. (195) The spectacle of the way people live in the world when bereft of associationship with holy men evokes tears. (18) Without worship, man's life is a poor thing, (160) a mere burden.

Mīrā cherished visual images of the beauty of the Lord in His manifest form as an adolescent boy (Kishor) in Gokul. She sings of his divine sports. She dances before His image in the temple. (36, 37) She drinks His footwash after Pūjā in the temple. (31) She ensconces His image in her heart. She longs to embrace His feet and be His personal servant. (94, 154, etc.) Whatever He clothes her in, that she wears. (20)

The path of devotion is difficult and the devotee finds unexpected obstructions. (54) Desire comes like a cur and imposes his fetters. (158) Pride is like a mountain on the slopes of which water will not settle. (158)

Mīrā was loyal to her aristocratic lineage in the very courage with which she rejected its customs. Her love was hidden at first, but later it expanded, like the seed of a banyan tree, for all to see. At the beginning of her love she might have restrained it. But once she was in mid stream there was no turning back. She follows the guidance of her Lord wherever it leads her, like a puppet attached to the thin thread of love. (173) She accepts praise or blame with equal humility and passes on. (13)

In one sense, Mīrā is ever conscious of the presence of her Lord within her heart. "Only she whose Beloved is abroad needs to write letters: my Beloved rests ever in my heart." (23) She has actually *seen* Him, present in her heart. (darasa lahyāṃ sukha-rāsī, Poem 194) Hence her every act is an act of worship. Wherever her feet touch the earth she is dancing in love of her Lord. (21) Yet the paradox holds that as long as worldly-life lasts He is both present and absent. The lover of God is he who, being awake to the presence of God, feels His absence, hidden by the world of multiplicity, all the more keenly. Shrī Chaturvedī quotes the Indian Sūfī poet Jāyasī, "The nectar of the sense of absence abides in love like honey in the honeycomb." Mīrā loves the Lord with the fidelity and loyalty of a young wife faced with the absence of her husband. (66) Only those who have felt the gash know the pain of love-wounds. (70 and 102) The sights and sounds of nature in spring or the rainy season only add to the pain.

Both the sense of the absence for the Lord and the awareness of His presence are capable of filling the devotee with such emotion that he is reduced to impotence. In the absence of her Lord, Mīrā wishes to write Him a letter, but her hand trembles and she is unable. Love is a state which reduces one to silence. The Gopīs distributing curds in pots are so carried away by the sight of Krishna that they cannot remember the word for curds. (177) But Mīrā dwells with particular insistence on the effect of the sense of the *absence* of the Beloved. It is felt so keenly as to induce a kind of madness (dīvānī, 70, 97, 130), involving an indifference to all worldly objects and values. A grain of Sufism seems to be detectable in Mīrā's mysticism, perhaps derived from her associationship with holy men of the Sant school, who themselves mingled with the Muslim mystics. She several times refers to her "darad", which prompts recall of a certain later Indian Sūfī poet (who was indeed known as "Dard") who said:

dard i dil ke wāste paidā kiyā insān ko
varanah tā'at ke liye kuch kam na the karūbiyāṃ

He created man to suffer agonies of the heart:
If it had only been a question of obedience,
There was not a scarcity of angels.

Mīrā predominantly worshipped God "with form" (saguṇa), and cannot without qualification be classed among the Sants. But her love is of the kind that demands and presupposes identity with its object, and when she emphasizes the identity-aspect her lines remind us not only of the Sants but sometimes even of the Upanishadic sages. Adoration of the beautiful Shyām is the dominant theme in her poetry, but the Beloved is Himself said to be "like the Indestructible Principle."(26) Mīrā is conscious of her identity with and separation from God at the same time. She can say "Thou and I are one like the sun and its heat" and "Come to my house, Thy coming will bring peace" in the same song. (114) She speaks mysteriously of an "impenetrable realm, that Death himself trembles to look upon." The phrasing of some lines in Mīrā suggests familiarity with and willingness to reproduce the teachings of Kabīr. (See Note 165 to Poem 158) In lines like "I care neither for Ganges nor Jumna, I am making my way to the sea" (Poem 24) we hear an echo of the ancient Upanishadic wisdom, through which the soul loses its individuality and unites in perfect identity with the supreme Spirit. She speaks of the body as a smock of five colours (the five elements) in which she is playing hide and seek with the Lord. Taking into account the traditions of Mīrā's childhood passion for the image of Krishna, and combining this with what we find in the Padāvalī, it is possible to think of Mīrā's devotion as developing through three stages. It can be seen as beginning with plain image-worship, progressing to the celebration of the glories of the Holy Avatāra Shrī Krishna in song and culminating in vision of Him as the Absolute beyond form. (Chaturvedī, Prem Sādhanā p. 139)

It seems that, throughout the history of the Indian spiritual quest from the Upanishads on, three tendencies can be noted. The first (with Shankara) locates the beginning of the path in devotion but tends to insist on the sole reality of the Absolute beyond all form and plurality and to preach knowledge as the only road to final release; the second insists on the validity of distinctions within the one all-comprehending reality, placing the ideal of perpetual adoration of God above the path of knowledge and tending to conceive the latter (with Vallabha) as a mere dissolution into the impersonal "unmanifest" aspect of the Lord (akshara, avyakta); the third insists that when either the path of devotion or the path of knowledge is followed to perfection the God to which they lead is the same. Āchārya Chaturvedī considers that Mīrā belonged to this last category, and quotes the following lines of Tulsī Dās as evincing a similar attitude. "There is no difference between (the Lord) with form and beyond form. So sing the Vedas and Purāṇas, the sages and enlightened souls. He who is attributeless, formless, unborn, transcendent—He it is who assumes manifest form, constrained by the love of His devotees." (Rāma Charita Mānasa I. cxv.1)

In Praise of the Lord

1

Worship the feet of Hari, O my mind,
Beautiful to look upon, soft and cool as a lotus,
Able to remove the three kinds of pain.[1]
When Prahlād grasped those holy feet
He was elevated to the rank of Indra.[2]
When Dhruv took refuge in them
He was transported to the motionless realm.[3]
In the fair body of the holy Dwarf
They measured the universe.[4]
Their touch saved the wife of Gautam.[5]
They tamed the serpent Kāliya
When Krishna sported as a cowherd.[6]
They supported the Govardhan Mountain
When Indra was put to shame.[7]
Mīrā is the servant of Lāl Giridhara,[8]
The raft on which to cross the unnavigable sea.[9]

2

I bow to Bihārī,[10]
Master of the arts of love.
His crown is a peacock's plume
And the tilak[11] gleams upon his brow.
His golden ear-rings and raven locks
Are waving gracefully at his ears.
He is playing the flute
That rests at His adorable lips.
Experiencing deep joy Himself,
He is charming the hearts of the women of Braj.[12]
On beholding this beautiful vision of Mohan[13] Giridhara,
Mīrā swoons in ecstasy.

Humble Petition

3

Come, take up Thy abode in my eyes,
O Son of Nand.[14]
Thy dark form is charming to look upon,
Thy lovely eyes loom large.
Thou hast applied the red tilak
And art wearing Thy crocodile ear-rings,
With Thy peacock-plume for a crown.
Thy necklace of gems [15] is hanging from Thy neck,
And there is Thy flute,
Spreading forth nectar from Thy holy lips.
Thy belt is adorned with small bells,
And the jingling of Thy anklets charms the heart.
Mīrā's Lord is Gopāl,[16]
He who watches over His devotees with love
And delights the hearts of holy men.

4

O Hari![17] Thou art the support of my life!
I have no other refuge but Thee
In all the three worlds.[18]
Though I have searched the whole universe,
Nothing pleases me but Thou.
Says Mīrā, "O Lord, I am Thy slave.
Do not forget me."

5

Deign to favour me, O Hari,
With the gift of a single glance.
My gaze is ever fixed on Thee,
But Thine is withdrawn.
Hard indeed must be Thy heart.
All my hopes are fixed
On receiving a single glance;
I have no other refuge whatever.

I am standing before Thee in supplication,
And behold! The dawn has come.
Mīrā's Lord is Hari, the Indestructible:[19]
To Him would she sacrifice her life.

Songs of Love

6

My Lord is that Brajavāsī[20] of Gokul.
All the inhabitants of Braj
Feel deep joy at the sight of the Divine Sports,
And the women are enraptured.
All dance and sing and clap their hands
And laugh for joy.
Now the merits of Nand and Yashodā
Arising from pious deeds in former births
Have come to fruition,
And the Lord, the Indestructible, has come.
He wears His yellow loin-cloth,
His necklace of gems hangs upon His chest
And He holds the fair flute in His hands.
Mīrā's Lord is the courtly[21] Giridhara.
May He grant unto His servant
His holy sight.

7

Sister, Shyām[22] smiles
And gazes at my body with His lustrous eyes.
His eyebrows are the bow,
And His side-long glances the arrows
Which strike against my heart.
Come, says my companion, heal thyself.
See, I will draw a yantra[23]
And affix it to thy body;
I will crush herbs and bring them for Thee.
But if thou art smitten with the disease of love
Such remedies will not avail.

How can I heal myself, O my companion?
I may crush cool sandalpaste and apply it,
I may resort to the magic of yantra and mantra,[24]
But that sweet image has entered my heart
And the damage is done.
Bring that Dark-Faced One before me,
I stand smiling in His expectation.
Pierce my body, look within
And see the broken fragments of my heart.
Without vision of her Lord Giridhara,
How can Mīrā continue to inhabit this house?[25]

8

O my companion, that impudent Son of Nand
Has made His abode in my heart.
He is holding the branch of a kadamba tree
And smiling gently in my direction.
His yellow loin-cloth reaches to His knees,
He wears a gem-studded crown upon His brow,
Mīrā's Lord is the courtly Giridhara,
Her mind is entrapped by His form.

9

Having beheld Thy beauty
I am caught and enmeshed.
My family members repeatedly try to restrain me,
But attachment to the Dancer with the Peacock Plume
Has now sunk deep.
My mind is drowned in the beauty of Shyām,
And the world says I have gone astray.
Mīrā has taken refuge with the Lord
Who knows the contents of every heart.

10

My eyes are spell-bound
By the beauty of the angular pose[26] of the Lord.
On beholding the beauty of Madan,[27]

My eyes drink in the nectar
And do not blink.
Attracted by the lotus-petal beauty of His brows,
It is as if they were now entangled
In His curling, odorous locks.
His body is bent at the waist,
His hands curved over the flute,
His turban is aslant and His necklace swinging.
Mīrā is thrilled by the beauty of the Lord,
Of the courtly Giridhara, dressed as a dancer.

11

I am utterly charmed by Mohan's beauty,
His beautiful body, His lotus-petal eyes,
His side-long glances, His gentle smiles.
He grazes His cows by the Yamunā,[28]
Playing sweetly on His flute.
I sacrifice to Giridhara
Body, mind, wealth and all.
Mīrā is hugging closely those lotus feet.

12

O my companion,
I have beheld Shyām, the Son of Nand.
I have lost all consciousness of my surroundings
And worldly shame has fled.
How beautiful are the crescent moons
Shimmering on His peacock-plume crown!
He wears a tilak-mark of saffron
Set between His lovely eyes.
His crocodile-earrings are glinting by His cheeks,
And His dark locks, playing in the breeze,
Look like fish rising up from a lake
To greet those monsters of the deep.
The Lord wears the garb of a dancer
And His beauty has charmed the whole world.
Mīrā would sacrifice her all
To every limb of the Lord Giridhara.

13

Once they are fixed upon the Lord
My thirsty eyes do not waver.
They drink in every atom of His body,
Ranging with anxious longing
From head to toe.
I was standing at the door of my house
When Mohan passed.
He was smiling gently,
His face radiant as the moon.
My relatives reproach me and crack bitter jests,
But my wayward eyes brook no obstruction.
They are sold and belong to another.
Whether they praise me or chide me,
I accept whatever is said
And raise it reverently to my forehead.
Says Mīrā: "Without my Master, Giridhara,
I cannot exist for a second."

14

O my companion,
Strange is the behaviour of my eyes.
That sweet form has entered my mind
And pierced its way into my heart.
How long have I been standing in my house
Gazing down the road?
My very existence depends on Shyām, the Beloved.
He is the herb that grants me life.
Mīrā has become the personal property of Giridhara:
The people say she is mad.

Love's Aspirations

15

O my companion, I will instal
That lotus-like figure in my eyes.

Now Shyām has come
And I dare not blink.
Murāri[29] has come to dwell in my heart,
Every instant I enjoy His sight.
I adorn myself to receive Shyām
And prepare a bed for His enjoyment.
Mīrā's Lord is the courtly Giridhara,
Again and again she offers Him her all.

16

Do not lose hold of such a gracious Master!
Offer thy body, mind and wealth
To Him alone.
Cherish His image in thy heart.
Come, my companion, look at His face,
Drink in the beauty with thine eyes.
Act only to please Him, in every way.
Shyām is lovely to look upon,
On a glimpse of His visage I live.
Krishna[30] is Mīrā's Lord.
Fortunate is she to have found His favour.

17

I danced before my Giridhara.
Again and again I dance
To please that discerning critic,
And put His former love to the test.
I put on the anklets
Of the love of Shyām,
And behold! My Mohan stays true.
Worldly shame and family custom
I have cast to the winds.
I do not forget the beauty of the Beloved
Even for an instant.
Mīrā is dyed deeply in the dye of Hari.

My Sole Support

18

My love is reserved for Giridhara Gopal[31]
And for no-one else.
O ye saints and holy men,
I have seen the world and its ways.
I left brothers and relatives
And all I possessed.
Dispensing with worldly shame,
I came to sit with the holy men.
I felt joy in the company of the devotees,
On beholding the world I wept.
I planted the creeper of love
And watered it with my tears.
I churned the curds
And drew forth the ghee:
The butter-milk I rejected.
The King sent me a cup of poison,[32]
I drank it down with joy.
Mīrā's love has set in deeply,
She accepts whatever comes.

19

O my companion,
I am dyed deep in the love of Shyām.
I have donned anklets and ornaments
And danced before Him without shame.
Now I keep company with the devout
And evil thoughts no longer assail me.
Love of Shyām is the one true thing
In all the world.
Night and day
Have I sung the glories of Hari :
I escaped from the black serpent.[33]
Without Shyām the world would be a desert,
And all worldly talk is vain and insipid.
Mīrā well knows the delights of devotion
To that courtly Giridhara, robed as a dancer.

20

Let me go to the house of Giridhara.
Giridhara is my true lover:
On beholding His beauty, I long for Him much.
As night falls I set out to see Him
And at break of day I return.
Day and night I sport in His company,
I please Him in any way I can.
Whatever He clothes me in, that I wear.
Whatever He offers, that I eat.[33a]
My love for Him
Is ancient and long-standing.[34]
Without Him I could not live.
Wherever He places me, there I remain.
If He sold me into slavery,
I would acquiesce.
Mīrā's Lord is the courtly Giridhara,
She offers herself in sacrifice again and again.

21

O my companion, all I can see[35] is Shyām,
All I can think of is Shyām.
Wherever my feet tread the earth
I am dancing in his honour.
Mīrā's Lord is the courtly Giridhara:
In His company
She is walking the woods and lanes.[36]

22

Sister, I have bought Govind in the market.
You only speak of it secretly,
But I proclaim it openly, beating a drum.
You say it was expensive,
But I say it was cheap,
And I measured it out on the scales.
I would offer my body,
I would offer my life,

For a prize beyond all price.
O Lord of Mīrā, grant her Thy sight
According to Thy promise in her former birth.[37]

23

I am dyed in the love of Giridhara,
My Beloved.
O my companion,
I am playing hide and seek with Him,
Robed in this smock of five colours.[38]
Disguised as I was, He caught me,
And on beholding His beauty
I made myself over to Him,
Body and soul.
Only she whose Beloved is abroad
Needs to write letters.
My Beloved rests ever in my heart,
He neither comes nor goes.
Mīrā's Lord is the courtly Giridhara.
She awaits Him fervently, night and day.

24

I have turned my back on this palace[39]
Once and for all,
And the bolt is drawn.
My good deeds in former births
Have come to fruition.
I have no use even for great lakes,
Who would linger over small ponds and reservoirs?
I care neither for Ganges nor Jamna,
I am making my way to the sea.
I do not need worldly associationships,
I have access to the true masters.
I will not trouble with the officials,
I will go direct to the court.
I, who beat iron with a sledge-hammer,
Am not concerned with pewter and glass.

I trade in diamonds
And do not care for gold and silver.
To my very great good fortune
A mine of precious stones is at hand.
Who would forsake a cup of nectar
To drink brackish water?
My Lord,
Now I have made acquaintance with Thy devotees
And shun the world from afar.
Mīrā's Lord is the courtly Giridhara:
He has fulfilled her desires.

My Own Path

25

Mīrā is dyed deep in the love of Hari
And all else is blocked out.
I wear only bangles, tilak and beads:
Beyond this, my only further ornament
Is my virtuous life.
No other embellishments please me,
Such was the wisdom
I received from my Teacher.
Some may revile me, others may praise me,
But I will only sing the glories of Govind.[40]
Wheresoever Krishna leads,
Thither will I follow.
I will not steal,
I will harm no one,
How can anyone touch me?
I will not descend
From the back of an elephant
To ride upon an ass.

26

Come sport with me here, my companions,
And refrain from visiting the houses of others.

False are rubies and pearls,
False all glamour and glimmer.
False is all external finery,
One's only real necklace
Is love of the Lord.
False are the silks of the south,
But the rags
Of love of the Lord are true,
For in them the body stays pure.
Eschew rich food
Cooked in the fifty-six kinds of condiments.
Flawed are all such enjoyments,
But the simple diet
Of love of one's Lord
Is good, cooked with salt or saltless.
Do not envy the orchards of another;
Till thine own poor plot
And good things will come of it.
If someone else
Has a rich and handsome husband,
It is nothing to do with thee.
If you seek his society
No one will approve.
It is good to remain loyal
To one's own husband,
Even if he be poor and a leper,
On this all are agreed.
My Beloved is like the Indestructible Principle,
Love of Him is true love.
The Lord has revealed Himself to Mīrā:
This is the path of true devotion.

Differences of Opinion Among Friends

27

Sister, the Lord of the Poor
Came to wed me in a dream.

Fifty-six crores of deities formed the bridal procession
And the bridegroom was the Lord of Braj.
In my dream,
I saw the wedding-arch constructed
And the Lord took my hand.
In my dream,
I underwent a wedding-ceremony
And entered the married state.
Giridhara has revealed Himself to Mīrā:
Her fortunes stem
From good deeds in past births.

28

Do not restrain me, my companion,
I am going to visit the holy men.
Shyām's form
Has come to dwell in my heart,
And I care for no other.
All the world is sleeping happily,
But my eyes are awake.
Mad and bereft of all insight,
Is he who rejects my Shyām,
Shyām invades my heart
And I cannot sleep.
No one drinks water
From the puddles that spring up
In the rainy months;
But Hari is a perpetual fountain of nectar,
Which quenches my thirst.
Beautiful is Shyām,
I am leaving now to gaze upon His face.
Mīrā is but a bewildered abandoned girl.
Come, accept her as Thine own.

Opposition

29

Though He is forbidden to me,
I cannot do without Shyām.
I will keep far away from the world
And enjoy the company of holy men
And the bliss of Hari.
He can take my body and mind,
As He already has my head.
My mind is fixed on Giridhara
And cares not for the insults of the world.
Mīrā's Lord is Hari, the Indestructible.
She says: I have taken refuge with Thee.

30

O King![41] Today I was very fortunate
And enjoyed the company of holy men.
Those who associate with holy men
Increase their devotion four-fold.
Do not associate with the Shāktas,[42]
It will interfere with your devotion.
All sixty-eight places of pilgrimage
Reside at the feet of a holy man,
Along with Banaras and the Ganges
Ten million times over.
Whoso abuses a holy man will go blind,
Be crippled and end in hell.
Mīrā's Lord is the courtly Giridhara
She says: I cover my limbs
With the dust of the feet of holy men.

31

Sister, I will sing the glories of Govind.
I will rise regularly at dawn
And go to the temple to have His sight,
And drink the water that has washed His feet.

I will dance in the temple of Hari,
Making my anklets jingle.
I will sail the boat of the Name of Shyām
And cross the Ocean of Becoming.
This world is a thorny briar-bush
And the road to the Beloved is blocked.
Mīrā's Lord is the courtly Giridhara.
She will reach Him through singing His glories.

Plain Speaking

32

Your gorgeous kingdom does not please me.
O King, there are no holy men in thy kingdom,
All are liars and good-for-nothings.
I have given up all my ornaments,
Even my bangles, O King.
I do not plait my hair
Or apply ointment to my eyes.
Mīrā's Lord is the courtly Giridhara,
She has found the perfect bridegroom.

33

O my King,
I relish this loss of good name greatly.
Some will revile me, some will praise me,
But I shall follow my unfathomable path.
On this narrow path
I have met men of God;[43]
Why turn back and abandon my unfathomable path ?
In the company of holy men
I have heard spiritual teaching.
Evil ones saw me and looked on.
Mīrā's Lord is the courtly Giridhara:
Let the evil ones burn up with hatred,
Like coals in a brazier.

34

O my King,
Why did you bear enmity against me?
Why do you play the prickly cactus?
Now I have left the palace
And its lofty towers.
I no longer live in your city.
I have renounced antimony and tilak
And donned the ochre robe.
Mīrā's Lord is the courtly Giridhara;
He turned the poison into nectar.

35

Sister,
If the King of the House of Sisodiyā[44] rages
What can he do?
I shall continue to sing the glories of Govind.
If the King become angry
He may keep his kingdom, and welcome;[45]
But if Hari becomes angry
I shall lose lustre like a withering flower.
I do not observe the rules of worldly decorum.
Fearlessly, Sister will I beat the drum.
O my companion, I will sail the boat
Of the Name of Shyām
And cross the Ocean of Becoming.
Mīrā has taken refuge with the dusky Giridhara;
Sister, she will keep close to those lotus feet.

36

I donned anklets and danced.
The people said "Mīrā is mad."
My mother-in-law declared
That I had ruined the family's reputation.
The King sent me a cup of poison
Which I drank with a smile.
I have offered body and mind

To the feet of Hari,
And will drink the nectar of His holy sight.
Mīrā's Lord is the courtly Giridhara:
My Lord, to Thee[46] will I go for refuge.

Testing

37

I am dyed deep in the love of Shyām,
My King, dyed deep in the love of Shyām.
I danced before the holy men,
Beating the drum.
People think I[47] am mad over Madan,
That love of Shyām has driven me silly.
The King sent me a cup of poison
Which I gulped down without even a look.
Mīrā's Lord is the courtly Giridhara,
His love is true, birth after birth.

38

I knew the Queen[47a] had sent me poison.
When gold is placed in fire
It emerges shining like the sun.
I have thrown away worldly shame
As one throws away dirty water.
You observe purdah in your place, my Queen,
But I am just a poor mad girl.
An arrow from the quiver of love
Has pierced my heart and driven me crazy.
I offer my body and mind
As a sacrifice to all holy men,
And I hug closely those lotus feet.
The Lord has taken[48] Mīrā into his protection,
Knowing her to be His servant.

39

Sister, I will sing the glories of Govind.
If the King shows displeasure
I can leave his kingdom,
But if Hari shows displeasure
Whither can I retreat?
The King sent me a cup of poison
And I accepted it as nectar,
As the very foot-wash of the Lord.[49]
He sent me a black serpent,
Hidden in a basket,
And I worshipped it
As the black stone that embodies Vishnu.[50]
Now Mīrā has gone veritably mad with love,
She has obtained Shyām for her bridegroom.

40

This love, Sister, is a love that endures.
I have drunk from the cup of nectar
And it has set me in a spin.
They cannot sober me, however they try.
The King sent a snake in a basket
And they gave it to the Princess of Meratā[51]
To put on her neck.
Mīrā donned it smiling,
Thinking "This is my best necklace."[52]
The King prepared a cup of poison
Which they gave to the princess to drink.
She drank it up
Like the foot-wash of the Lord,
Singing the glories of Govind.
I have drunk from the cup
Of the Holy Name,
And nothing else pleases me.
Mīrā's Lord is the courtly Giridhara,
His love is paint that does not peel.

41

Mīrā has been singing the glories of Govind
And is immersed in joy.
The King sent a snake in a basket:
They came and placed it in Mīrā's hand.
I washed and came to look at it,
And behold!
It was the Black Stone of Vishnu.[53]
The King sent a cup of poison,
But my Lord converted it into nectar.
When I washed my hand and drank,
Behold! It was nectar.
The King sent a mattress of thorns,
Saying: "Give that to Mīrā to sleep upon."
When evening came and Mīrā lay down,
Behold! It was a bed of flowers.
Mīrā's Lord ever stands as her helper
And preserves her from dangers.
She wanders about recklessly,
Drunk in adoration,
Offering herself to Giridhara in total sacrifice.

42

O Sister, without Hari I cannot live.
My mother-in-law fights with me,
My sister-in-law scolds me,
The King is permanently in a rage.
They have bolted my door
And mounted a guard outside it.
Why should I abandon my ancient love
Inherited from earlier births?
Mīrā's Lord is the courtly Giridhara
And she will be satisfied with nothing else.

Sufferings in Absence

43

I do not know how to meet my Lord.
He came into my courtyard and went,
And I only know that I missed Him.
I spend days in search,
Scanning the road night and day.
Hari came into my courtyard,
But, wretch that I am,
I was asleep.
The pain of absence burns my bewildered heart
And gives me no rest.
O Servant Mīrā,
Whoso once meets Lāl Giridhara
Should never let go.

44

O Jogī,[54] I scan the road
Searching for Thee day and night.
My feet will not tread the difficult path:
It is strange, and has many pitfalls.
A Jogī came to the city,
But found not love in my heart and left.
Artless as I was,
I failed to entrap and hold Him.
Since then I have searched for many days,
But still He has not returned.
Come and quench the longing in my heart,
A veritable fire is raging in my body.
Either the Jogī is no longer alive
Or else He has forgotten me completely.
What can I do? where shall I go?
Sister, tears have rendered my eyes useless.
My Lord, I long for Thee in my heart,
Come, knowing me to be Thine.
Mīrā feels abandoned and perplexed.
Without Thee, she can only pant and sigh.

45

My thirsty eyes are longiing for His sight.
Whole days have I passed, Sister,
In scanning the road.
The pain in my eyes is great.
A cuckoo has been singing from a branch,
And its song has pierced me deeply.[55]
The elders speak bitter words
And crack jokes at my expense.
But Mīrā is sold into Hari's hands,
His slave for birth upon birth.

46

O Jogī, do not depart,
I pray you, do not depart.
Behold, I fall at Your feet, Your slave.
Strange is the path of love and devotion!
Explain to me its intricacies
Before You depart.
I am laying a pyre of fragrant aloe
And sandalwood.
Light it with Your own hand
Before You depart.
When I am burnt to a heap of ashes,
Smear them on Your body
Before You depart.
Says Mīrā to her Lord, the courtly Giridhara,
Let my light dissolve in Your light
Before You depart.

47

O Giridhara Lāl, You enjoyed a feast.
Servant Mīrā begged a boon,
And my dear Krishna showed His compassion.
He who protects and nourishes His servants
Accepted a savoury dish.
I held the platter before Him

While Giridhara feasted royally.
Servant Mīrā will take refuge with Thee,
Grant her contentment soon.

48

Do not go off and abandon me, my Lord.
Weak woman as I am,
Giridhara is my strength.
He is my Master.
I am quite without merit
While Giridhara possesses every virtue.
His presence bejewels my heart.
You are the Saviour of the World
And the remover of all affliction.
You came to the rescue of the elephant.[56]
I place my ruined life
In the shadow of Your protection.
Where else could I go, O King of Braj?
Mīrā recognizes no other Master,
Now spare her from further ignominy.

49

Where are You going,
Having lit the flames of love?
Without Your sight I enjoy no repose,
Life is suffocating and will not last.
I will become a wandering Joginī
For Your sake,
Or end my life beneath the saw of Kāshī.[57]

50

O my Beloved, stay before my eyes.
Do not forget me,
I am drowning in the Ocean of Becoming,
Remember me soon.
The King has sent me a cup of poison,

Grant the boon that it may become nectar.
Mīrā's Lord is the courtly Girdhara,
Do not leave me when once we have met.

51

What shall I say to you,
O my Shyām Giridhara?
My love is ancient
And runs from former births,
Do not abandon me, Giridhara.
I offer myself in unconditional sacrifice, my darling,
When I behold Thy beautiful face.
Come into my courtyard, Giridhara,
The women are singing auspicious hymns.
I have set aside a square for Thy welcome,
Heaped with the pearls of my tears.
I cast myself before Thee, body and mind.
Servant Mīrā takes refuge at Thy feet:
For Thy sake she has remained a virgin
From birth to birth.

Reproaches

52

Sister, behold how Hari has hardened His heart!
He said He would come,
But has not done so.
That was His promise when He went.
Food, drink and my surroundings,
Are all forgotten.
Why does my life go on?
Thy actions belie Thy words, my Master,
How couldst Thou have forgotten me?
Mīrā's Lord is the courtly Giridhara.
She says: Without Thee I am heart-broken.

53

To fall in love with a Jogī
Is to court pain.
I loved, but it has brought me no joy,
My sister.
The Jogī befriends no one.
Until I meet Thee again,
I shall have no rest, day or night.
Never again in this world
Have I beheld beauty like Thine.
Mīrā says: My Lord, when shall we meet?
Great will be the joy of that meeting.

54

To love a Jogī brings pain.
He speaks sweet words
When you are with him,
But then He forgets you and goes.
Sister, He snaps the ties of love
As you might pluck a sprig of jasmine.
Says Mīrā: My Lord,
Without Thy sight my heart grieves sorely.

55

One day, perhaps, you will remember me,
My wandering Krishna,[58] so aloof.
You took up your seat
In motionless contemplation,
As is proper on the path of devotion.
I thought You would take me when You went,
But You left me behind in the lurch.
You do not see a Jogī come,
You do not see him go.
Who can say that a Jogī is his friend?
Says Mīrā: O my courtly Giridhara,
My mind has gone to your feet.

56

O Mohan, I know your ways of love,
Know them well.
Mine is the Path of Love and Devotion,
I know no other.
Why, having first plied me with nectar,
Do you serve me with poison now?
Where did you learn manners like this?
Mīrā's Lord is Hari, the Indestructible.
He is the true friend of His devotees.

57

Let Him go, let Him go, my companion!
To whom is a Jogī a friend?
He remains ever indifferent to me,
Utterly peculiar in his behaviour.
He seems to speak sweetly,
But never gives His love.
I thought the affair would succeed,
But He left me[59] half-way and went off.
Mīrā's Lord is the delightful Shyām,
Dear because the object of her love!

58

Come, Jogī, smile and talk,
Your lofty indifference[60] is a sham.
I've told the whole world now, Manamohan,[61]
To the beat of a drum.
Come, You with the deer-skin
And the ash-smeared body—
Just tell the people the truth.
Thy face has the beauty of a new-born[62] lotus,
I stand and gaze at Thy cheeks.
I have neither beads, nor ashes,
Nor horn nor selī.[63]
Open Thy mouth, O Silent One.
Do not wander from door to door,

Flaunting Thy youth and piercing eyes.[64]
Mīrā's Lord is Hari, the Indestructible
She has sold herself in slavery to Him
Without accepting a fee.

59

O Krishna,[65] O All-Pervading One,
My love is for Thee alone.
When love has once set in, my dearest,
Do not break it off,
But go on increasing Thy affection instead.
Had I known what pain arose from love,
My dearest,
I would have proclaimed "Let no one love"
All over the town with an enormous drum.
Do not make friends with fools:
Sister, leave that treacherous dish alone.[66]
Now they are warm, now cold,
Now your accomplice, now your enemy.
To love is madness:
But those who, having once given their love,
Retract it later, are cruel.
He is a rare hero who loves on,
Trampling all opposition underfoot.
Thou art strong like a well-cemented terrace,
And I am weak like a wall of sand.
How can I now revive that love
I enjoyed in former births?
You may plant in the same place
A mango and an acacia,
But the one will still yield a sweet drink
And the other thorns.
Love with the fickle-minded
Is like a thin stream descending from a height:
It flows freely and froths much
But soon announces its exhaustion.[67]
Now the rainy months have come
And the cry of the peacock is heard.

Caught in the puffs of a divine breeze
Mīrā has been wafted away
To join the devotees of Hari.[68]

60

O Giridhara,
Why hast Thou become angry with me?
Recount some of my faults,
I am eager to hear.
I have been Thy slave for many births
And Thou art my excellent Master.
Says Mīrā: O my Lord,
O Giridhara the courtly one,
I take Thy Name and Thine alone.

Hymns of Praise

61

Hari,
Thou didst remove the afflictions of Thy devotees.
Thou didst spare the shame of Draupadī[69]
By continually lengthening her dress.
Thou didst assume the form of a Man-Lion
To save Thy devotee Prahlād.[70]
Thou didst save the Elephant from drowning.[71]
Mīrā is the servant of Lāl Giridhara:
He has removed[72] all my afflictions.

62

Take my arm immediately,
If only to preserve Thine own reputation.
O Giridhara they call Thee
The Refuge of the Afflicted.
Thou hast promised to save the fallen.
I am plunged in the ocean of transmigration
Without a support.

Without Thee, I shall suffer a mighty disaster.
Thou savest Thy devotees from their afflictions
In every age,
Appearing before them to grant them release.[73]
Mīrā has taken refuge with Thee,
And is grasping Thy feet
Redeem Thy pledge,[74] O King.

63

Without Hari, behold my wretched condition.
They say that Thou art my protector
And I Thy servant.
I have practised remembrance of Thy Name
In my heart, day and night.
Again and again I call upon Thee,
In grievous affliction.
This world is a threatening sea,
Surrounding me on every side.
My boat has broken,
Hoist the sail quickly
Before it sinks.
This forlorn one waits anxiously for her Lord,
Grant her Thy proximity.
Servant Mīrā repeats "Rām Rām!"[75]
I take refuge in Thee alone.

64

My Lord, You have inspired me with love,
Where have You now gone?
You have abandoned me, Your faithful companion,
Having lit the flame of love.
You have set the boat of love in motion
And abandoned it on the ocean of longing.
My Lord, when can I meet You?
Without You, I cannot survive.

65

The Charmer of Hearts has gone,
Having caught me in the noose of love.

On the bough of a mango tree
A cuckoo is pouring forth her plaintive song.
The world just laughs,
But for me it is death.
I tramp the forests
In desolation at the absence of the Beloved.
Let me die,
Let me perish in the saw at Kāshī.[76]
Mīrā's Lord is Hari, the Indestructible.
Thou art my Master and I Thy servant.

66

Sister, Hari will not speak to me,
Why does not my wretched breath
Abandon my body?
The night passed
And I neither removed my veil nor spoke.[77]
An age has passed without converse,
How can I prosper in conditions like this?
I heard that Hari would come in the rainy season.
The nights were thick with darkness,
Lightning flashed
And I would count the hours till dawn.
Servant Mīrā is dyed in the love of Shyām:
Her whole life passes in longing.

67

I am invaded by memories
Of the conduct of the supremely affectionate Krishna.[78]
Krishna belongs to me
And I belong to Him:
Without Him, nothing pleases me.
He said He would come but has not appeared,
My heart is deeply distraught.
My only desire, O Krishna,
Is to enjoy vision of Thee.
When will Hari grant me His holy sight?

Deep is my love for those lotus feet,
And without His sight I suffer greatly.
When Mīrā's Lord grants her His sight
Her joy will be beyond description.

68

My darkling Beloved has gone abroad.
My lost one has not returned
Or even sent me a message.
I have put off my jewelry
And shaved my hair.
For Thy sake have I donned the orange robe
And gone forth searching the four quarters.
Says Mīrā: O my Lord Shyām,
Unless I can be with Thee,
My birth and life are but an affliction.

69

O my companion,
Without Shyām I cannot survive.
Charmed by Thy beauty, O my Beloved,
I offer Thee my body, mind and life.
I have lost all appetite for food and drink
And my eyes have gone dim.
O Murāri,[79] day and night
I dream of meeting Thee,
When shall I have Thy sight?
Days and nights pass
As I call upon Thee.
Says Mīrā: O Hari,
Without Thee my life flickers feebly on.

70

I am mad with love
And no one understands my plight.
Only the wounded
Understand the agonies of the wounded,

When a fire rages in the heart.
Only the jeweller knows the value of the jewel,
Not the one who lets it go.[80]
In pain I wandered from door to door,
But could not find a doctor.
Says Mīrā: Harken, my Master,
Mīrā's pain will subside
When Shyām comes as the doctor.

71

Without my beloved Master
I cannot live.
Body, mind and life
Have I given to the Beloved.
Fascinated by His beauty,
I gaze down the road
Night and day.
Says Mīrā: My Lord, accept your servant—
It is all she asks.[81]

72

The link between me and Shyām
Cannot be broken.
I went yellow as the autumn leaf
And the people thought I had jaundice.
My father [82] sent for the doctor,
Who felt my pulse.
It was my heart that was breaking,
But the doctor did not know the secret.
My Lord, Mīrā is distressed in Your absence,
Come and grant her Your sight.

73

Who can understand the grief
Of a woman parted from her beloved?
Only one who has felt the pangs of absence,
Or perhaps a devotee.

The physician is present within the patient:
Only the physician knows the remedy.
The dagger[83] of the absence of the Beloved
Has pierced my breast:
Without Hari, all pleasures are as dust.
I am like a mad cow roaming the forest,
Who can think only of her lost calf.
The Chātak dreams of the rain of Swātī,[84]
Crying "Lord, Lord"[85] in great distress.
The world is all thorns,
A veritable garbage-heap,
And no one sees my pain.
Krishna is Mīrā's Lord and Master:
She could not find another if she sought.[86]

74

Without Krishna I cannot sleep.
Tortured by longing, I cannot sleep,
And the fire of love
Drives me to wander hither and thither.
Without the light of the Beloved
My house is dark,
And lamps do not please me.
Without the Beloved my bed is uninviting,
And I pass the nights awake.
When will my Beloved return home?
The frogs are croaking, the peacock's cry
And the cuckoo's song are heard.
Low black clouds are gathering,
Lightning flashes, stirring fear in the heart.
My eyes fill with tears.
What shall I do? Where shall I go?
Who can quench my pain?
My body has been bitten
By the snake of "absence",
And my life is ebbing away
With every beat of the heart.
Fetch the herb quickly.

Which of my companions
Will come bringing the Beloved to meet me?
My Lord when will you come
To meet your Mīrā?
Manamohan, the Charmer of Hearts,
Fills me with delight. When, my Lord,
Will you come to laugh and talk with me?

75

Sleep has not visited me the whole night,
Will the dawn ever come?
O my companion,
Once I awoke with a start from a dream.
Now the remembrance of that vision
Never fades.
My life is ebbing as I choke and sigh,
When will the Lord of the Afflicted come?
I have lost my senses and gone mad,
But the Lord knows my secret.
He who deals out life and death
Knows the secret of Mīrā's pain.

76

How can I finish a letter
When I cannot even write?
My hand trembles when I take up the pen
And my eyes flood with tears.
When I want to say anything
I cannot speak.
My heart is sore afraid.
You have beheld my plight.
Go to Hari, and beg of Mīrā's Lord,
The courtly Giridhara,
That He may keep a place for her
At His lotus feet.

77

In the absence of the Beloved
The sports of Holī[87] leave a bitter taste.

The whole village seems mournful,
Mournful one's bed and house.
This abandoned one wanders about mournfully
Without her Beloved.
The Beloved has left her and gone off,
Leaving her afflicted with the pain of absence.
Do not keep travelling from place to place,
My anxiety is heavy.
I have blurred the lines on my fingers
With counting. O Murāri,[88] come!
They are playing the flutes and drums
And the one-stringed lute.
Spring has come, but the Beloved has not.
My pain grows deeper;
Why have you forgotten me, Shyām?
O Giridhara, I stand before You in supplication.
Spare my shame.
Says Mīrā: O Mādhav,[89] O my Master,
For Thy sake have I preserved virginity
Birth after birth. Come to my side.
My mind has taken full refuge in Thee.[90]

78

I take no pleasure in Holī
Without the presence of my Beloved.
My house and its courtyard
Are alike repellent.
Sister, the place of honour in my house
Is filled with lamps[91]
To honour my distant Lord.
My empty bed seems like a snake.
Sleep will not come to my eyes,
How will the night pass?
How long have I been standing
Gazing down the road?
The pain of absence keeps me awake
Night and day.
To whom can I recount

The sufferings of my mind?
My heart remains uneasy,
When will the Beloved come?
I see no dear soul
Kind enough to take a message.
When will I have the chance
To smile and embrace the Beloved?
Then would Mīrā sing the songs of Holī.

80

The Beloved has abandoned me,
With whom could I play Holī?[92]
I have taken off all gems and pearls
And donned the yogī's beads.
Neither food nor house please me,
The Beloved has driven me mad.
Why did He subject me
To the pain of absence?
If You are now making love to another
Why did You make love to me first?
Many days have passed
And still He has not come.
O my companion, I am disturbed.
Who can be holding Him back?
Without Shyām my life-force shrivels and contracts
Like a plant with water.
O my Master,
Mīrā has been Thy servant birth after birth,
Grant her Thy sight.
Without Thy sight
She can only stand in sorrow.

81

See, the tumbling clouds hove come,
But they have not brought a message from Hari.
The songs of the frog, the peacock,
The papīhā and the koil are heard.
All is thick darkness

When suddenly the lightning flashes,
Causing great trepidation
To her whose Beloved is absent.
Thunder rolls,
A sweet, soft breeze sets in,
With steady rain.
Now the snake of "absence"
Bites really hard.
Hari has captured Mīrā's heart.

82

O Shyām, I saw a rain-cloud bursting,
And burst into tears myself.
The clouds massed black and yellow,
And rained for two hours on end.
Wherever I look there is water, water.
Green herbage has covered the thirsty earth.
My Beloved has gone abroad,
And I have become drenched
Standing at the door waiting for Him.
Mīrā says: O my Master, the eternal Hari,
Fulfil the obligations of sincere love.[93]

In the Throes of Longing

83

Whence arose those feelings of spite
That you suddenly remembered, O Papīhā ?[94]
I was sleeping in my house
When your cry came "Darling, darling".
It was salt on my wounds,
An axe[95] laid at my heart.
You were perched on the branch
Of a tall tree,
Singing at the top of your voice.
Mīrā's Lord is the courtly Giridhara,
She has laid her mind at His feet.

84

O Papīhā,
Do not call out for the Beloved.
If one in the throes of absence should hear you
She would twist off your wings
And throw them away.
I will get them to cut off your beak
And will pour black salt on the wound.
I belong to the Beloved
And He belongs to me alone.
Who are you to call Him "darling"?
Yet if I should meet the Beloved today
Your voice would sound sweet.
I would gild your beak
And make you my pet.
I will write the Beloved a letter.
Take it for me, friend crow.
Tell the Beloved
That His abandoned one is not eating.
Servant Mīrā is in distress,
Passing the time calling out for the Beloved.
Come quickly O Master, O Inner Ruler,
Without Thee I cannot survive.

85

O my companion,
My "Charmer of Hearts" has not come.
Perhaps he has taken up the life
Of a holy man.
Or has He simply forgotten the way?
What shall I do? Where shall I go?
Now the pain of absence is deeply disturbing.
Servant Mīrā is thirsty for Thy sight.
Her mind has gone to the feet of Hari.

86

I sit up awake while the world sleeps.
The abandoned one sits in the *pleasure-palace,*

Threading the pearls of her tears.
Just such an abandoned one once I saw
Threading a necklace from her tears.
I pass the night counting the stars
Awaiting the hours of joy.[96]
Mīrā says: O my Lord Giridhara,
Come, for this separation[97] must end.

87

Friend, I have lost all sleep.
I spend the whole night
Watching and waiting for the Beloved.
My companions came to lecture me,
But my mind would not listen.
Without seeing Him I cannot rest,
Yet I will not be angry.
My body is thin, I am greatly distracted,
My lips keep repeating the word "darling".
You did not understand
The agonies I suffered in separation,
The pain of my heart.
The chātak bird thinks only of the cloud,
The stranded fish thinks only of the sea.
Mīrā, too, is abandoned and distracted.
She has lost consciousness of her surroundings.

88

That dark form has entered my heart.
I meditate on Giridhara night and day,
And Mohan surely abides in my heart.
I am bitten by the snake of love of Shyām
And stand utterly bewildered.
Says Mīrā: O my Master,
When will You come ?
Every day finds me filled with love anew.

89

Sister, without the Lord I cannot carry on.
My life-force is failing,

Without Hari I cannot carry on.
The tortoise and the frog live in water,
And from water were they born.
But greater is the fish:
Take him from water and he immediately dies.
The log has fallen in the forest
And the weevils[98] are attacking it savagely.
But if the Lord came
And threw it into the fire,
Behold! It would burn to ashes.
I wander from wood to wood,
Hardly retaining consciousness.
Grant me Thy sight but once
And all my evils will cease.
I have turned yellow as a sear leaf
And am visited with sore pain.
O Lāl Giridhara, this is Thy servant Mīrā.
Through meeting Thee she has now found joy.

90

Sister! Without Hari, how can I live?
Without Shyām I have gone crazy,
My mind is like wood attacked by weevils.
The pain of love is devouring me
And no medicine avails.
When the fish is sundered from the water
It flaps feebly and dies.
I search endlessly for Shyām in the forests,
Drawn on by the sound of the flute.
Says Mīrā: O Lāl Giridhara, my Master,
Come quickly to my side.

91

My companion, a deep longing to meet Shyām
Has arisen within me.
I toss and turn and find no ease,
The fire of "absence" has set in.
I call out for the Beloved

Night and day, abandoning worldly shame
And family custom.
The snake of separation has bitten my heart,
And now it pumps jets of poison.
Mīrā is miserable and utterly bewildered,
Her desire for Shyām is deep.

92

Shyām, without Thee I cannot sleep.
Every second seems many an age,
Every moment I am tortured by separation.
Without the Beloved[99] I remain in darkness,
Neither lamps nor palaces please me.
A bed of flowers seems a bed of thorns
And I pass my nights awake.
To whom can I speak ?
Who would believe me ?
Who would have faith in my words ?
The Beloved is a snake
Who has bitten my hand,
And my life is ebbing with every pulse.
I hear the frog's croaking, the peacock's cry
And the song of the koil and papīhā.
Dark low clouds have gathered,
The lightning's flash inspires terror.
O Krishna,[100]
Is there any loving soul in the world
Who will ease my pain ?
Mīrā's Lord is Hari, the Indestructible.
His sight would refresh her eyes.

93

I have sacrificed my life
Unto the beautiful Shyām.
For Thy sake, O Shyām,
I have abandoned worldly shame and family custom.
Without His sight I find no rest
And streams of tears fall from my eyes.

To whom could I speak ?
Who could assuage my pain ?
The river of separation is a powerful stream.
Says Mīrā: Harken, Lord, grant me Thy sight,
For Thy feet are my only support.

94

O Shyām, hear my pitiful prayer.
I will remain Thy faithful servant.
I am mad with desire for Thy sight
And the plague of separation has attacked me.
For Thy sake I will become a Joginī
And wander from city to city.
I will seek Thee in every nook.
I will don ashes and deer-skin,
And will veritably reduce this body to ashes.
Krishna,[101] the Indestructible, has not yet come :
I will wander from wood to wood,
Weeping and calling out.
O Giridhara,
Come to the side of Thy devotee Mīrā,
It will end her pain and bring abundant joy.
Now there is peace in my breast,
Through and through.
My wanderings are at an end.
I shall remain at Thy feet,
Thy servant for ever.

95

Come straight away to my house,[102]
O my Beloved.
Thou art mine and I am Thine.
I, Thy devotee, await Thee expectantly,
Gazing eagerly down the road.
Time has passed,
And still Thou hast not come.
Hast Thou fallen in love
With my messenger ?[103]

Says Mīrā: O my Master,
When wilt Thou come?
Without Thy sight the days are hard.

96

Come to my house, O Lord of the Universe!
My body is in pain, my breath burning.
Come and extinguish the fire of separation.
I spend the nights roving about in tears.
Appetite and sleep have left me,
But my shameless life clings on.
Grant me happiness, do not desolate me.
Delay no longer,
Thy abandoned Mīrā is in sore straits.

97

O Jogī,
If You would but grant me Your sight,
Great would be my joy.
Otherwise life on earth is only pain,
A continuous suffering in Your absence,
Day and night.
My sufferings have driven me mad,
I have tramped the whole country through.
Mīrā has been Your true servant,
Now her black hair has turned white.

98

Come to my house, O Jogī,
With Thy ear-rings, Thy beads
And Thy ash-smeared body.
Without Thy sight I feel no rest.
I am happy neither in the house
Nor the courtyard.
Hari, the Indestructible, is Mīrā's Lord.
Come and grant me Thy sight.

99

Come, O Charmer of Hearts,
I am waiting expectantly.
I do not touch food or drink,
Nor do my eyelids close in sleep.
In Thy absence I can enjoy nothing
And my heart is deeply despondent.
Without Thee, Mīrā has gone demented.
Do not leave her supportless.

100

Come, Charmer of Hearts,
For Your speech is sweet.
O Krishna, did You ever rightly value
My childhood love ?
Without Your sight I feel no ease,
My mind swings this way and that.
Mīrā says: I am Yours.
I will proclaim this, with Your permission,
To the beat of a drum.

101

My darling, grant me Your sight,
I cannot exist without You.
Life without You
Is like a pond without a lotus,
Or a night without the moon.
I pass the nights in deep distress,
The pain of absence eats my heart.
No food by day, no sleep by night,
No words pass my lips either.
Who will listen to me ?
To whom can I speak ?
Come, my Beloved, and quench my pain.
Why do You torment me, O Inner Ruler ?
If You came, my pain would go.
Mīrā is Your servant,
Her Love[104] has run for many births.

102

Without Thy sight
I cannot rest a minute.
My house looks ugly,
Sleep deserts me,
And I am plagued by the sense of absence.
I wander about like a wounded thing
And no one knows my pain.
My life is ebbing, I wither,
My eyes are blurred with tears.
I stand and stand in expectation,
Gazing down Thy path.
Says Mīrā: When shall I meet You,
My Lord ? To meet You
Would bring joy.

103

Without Thy sight
Sorrow attends my eyes.
When I fancy I hear Thy words,
My heart trembles.
Sweet is Thy voice.
To whom can I explain my sufferings ?
I am being mangled in the jaws
Of the circular saw of "pain of absence".
O Hari, I gaze down Thy path,
I experience no peace
And a night seems like half a year.
I toss and turn in Thy absence
And peace and joy are gone.
Says Mīrā: My Lord, when will You come ?
Your coming will end my sorrows
And bring joy.

104

Why do You torment me ?
For Your sake I abandoned the world
And my family.

Why do You now forget me ?
You lit the fire of the pain of absence,
But You have not returned to put it out.
You cannot escape me now, Murāri,
I have come forward to grasp Your feet
Mīrā has been Thy slave for many births.
Thou hast promised to save Thy devotees,
Redeem Thy pledge.[105]

105

My love for Thee has set in deeply,
O courtly Son of Nand.[106]
Having heard the music of Thy flute
I have forgotten family and home.
When the fish is dying on the bank
The water knows nothing of its pain.
The moth is burnt to ashes
And the flame knows not its agonies.
Says Mīrā: O Shyām, my Master,
Without Thee I remain in embodied existence,
But can I be said to live ?[107]

106

Thou art my companion of many births,
I do not forget Thee day or night.
Without Thee I can enjoy no peace,
My heart knows it well.
I climbed a high place
To scan Thy path.
I suffered sorely and my eyes grew red.
False is the ocean of transmigration,
False is bondage to the world,
False all family ties.
I gaze at Thy form every moment
And feel the intoxication of Thy beauty.
Mīrā's Lord is the courtly Giridhara,
Her mind is dyed in the feet of Hari.

107

My beloved, think of me as Thou wilt,
I have no other refuge but Thee,
Grant me Thy grace.
I do not eat by day
Or sleep by night.
My body is wasting away every moment.
Mīrā's Lord is the courtly Giridhara.
Come to her,
And do not forsake her again.

108

Deep is my longing to meet with Shyām.
Every day I rise early
And wait for Him in expectation.
Many days have passed in torment,
I am caught in the net of longing.
Show me Thy compassion soon, my Master,
Am I not Thy slave ?
My weary eyes long for Thy sight,
My breath will hardly emerge from my body.[108]
Day and night my only thought is
"When will Hari keep me by His side ?"
Mine is a love that will not lapse,
Why do you still make mischief ?[109]
O Master of Mīrā,
When will You come ?
Your coming will fulfil all my desires.

109

Come to my house, my darling, my Beloved.
I will offer You my eyes
As a carpet to walk upon,
My heart as a couch,
And will seat You ensconced upon my head.
O my guest,
Thy coming will benefit me greatly,

For Thy mission is salvation from the world.
Thou hast rescued Thy devotees
From various evil plights,
And assured them the rewards
Of all their pious deeds.
Mīrā says: O my Master, the courtly Giridhara,
Grasp my arm and spare my shame.

110

O my companion,
When will my Beloved come?
Surely the lotus feet of the courtly Giridhara
Will grant me joy,
For I have fastened my eyes upon them.
Deep is my desire to see Thee,
To behold Thy face.
My wits are disturbed,
My very life insecure,
Come quickly to relieve my pain.
Says Mīrā: O my Master, the courtly Giridhara,
Without Thee my sufferings are great.

111

Think of me as Thou wilt,
I am gazing down Thy path
Every moment. Grant me Thy sight.
I am full of defects,
But consider not my defects.
I am a slave to Thy lotus feet,
Come to me and do not depart.
Says Mīrā: I have taken refuge
With the true Teacher,[110]
And have applied my mind
To the feet of Hari.

112

Come to my house, my Beloved, my dearest.
Without Thee, the whole world tastes bitter.

I will offer you my body, my mind
And my worldly possessions,
And will perform Thy worship.
Thou art a vast of ocean of virtues
And I a mass of defects.
I am worthless, without a single grace,
But Thou art forgiving.
Says Mīrā: My master, when will You come?
Without You my eyes feel sore pain.

113

O Krishna, offering myself completely in sacrifice,
I beg of You to come to my street.
Without Thy sight I feel no ease
And can only gaze down Thy path.
Who is Your new lady-love,
Dearer to You than I?
Be compassionate and grant me Thy sight,
Overlooking all my faults.
O Murāri, Thou art supremely compassionate
To those who take refuge at Thy feet.
Save me from the ocean of transmigration.
Mīrā is the slave of Thy feet.
She offers herself in sacrifice again and again.

114

Come to my house, O Krishna,
Thy coming will bring peace.
Great will be my joy if I meet Thee,
And all my desires will be fulfilled.
Thou and I are one,
Like the sun and its heat.
Mīrā's heart cares for nothing else,
It only wants the beautiful Shyām.

115

O Beloved, grant me Thy sight.
Again and again I call out to Thee,

Grant me Thy grace.
In the hot weather of late May
The land is dessicated, the birds suffer.
As May gives way to June,
The peacock cries out piteously
And the cuckoo wails for the clouds.
When the rains set in,
The women observe the Tīj festival.
In the month of Bhādon
The rivers swirl—
No one absents themselves then.[111]
In the month of Kwār,
The oyster-shells hanker for rain.[112]
In the month of Kārttik
People worship in the temple,
But in my case,
Thou art my only divinity.
Cold are the days of Mārgashīrsh,
So come quickly to protect me.
In the month of Paush
The earth is covered with thick frost,
Come Yourself to see it.
In the month of Māgh
They celebrate Vasant Panchamī.
In Phālgun they sing songs.
They celebrate Holī with mirth and games
And burn whole woods in bonfires.
In the month of Chaitra
Longing rises in the heart—
Grant me Thy sight.
In the month of Vaishākh
The trees burst into blossom,
And the cuckoo sings his plaintive song.
The day has passed in driving off crows[113]
And I have also consulted the astrologers.
Mīrā is abandoned and miserable.
When will she have His sight?[113]

116

O Jogī, come to this land.
Let me see Thee with my eyes,
And run to prostrate before Thee
With my humble petition.
The rainy season has come,
Dry land, rivers and tanks
Are all flooded.
Who is holding You back,
A prisoner of love?
Your abandoned one is deeply distraught.
The rainy season is now long over,
But nothing hinders my power to weep.
Just alter direction
And come to our city.
That beautiful form
Has taken up its station in my heart,
And I can hardly live any longer.
Mīrā has no other possession but Thee:
Come to her and grant her Thy sight.

117

Take my humble petition to the Jogī.
O my companion, the Jogī is very wise.
Even Shiv and Shesh[115] meditate upon Him.
I will come! I will not remain
In a distant place, parted from the Beloved.
O my protector, be gracious
And keep me by Thy side.[116]
My Dearest,
I will don the beads, ear-rings and belt,
And will take the begging-bowl in my hands.
I will become a wandering Joginī,
And will search long ages
Till I enjoy Thy presence at last.
The Beloved said He would come
In the rainy season.
He made many promises,

But I have blurred the lines on my fingers
Counting the days.
I have fallen yellow, my Dearest,
On account of the absence of the Beloved,
A strange livery for a girl in her youth.
Servant Mīrā, having worshipped Krishna,
Has offered Him her body and mind.

118

How long have I been standing
Waiting expectantly and ready for service?
Deign to vouchsafe me a glance,
O Friend of the Afflicted.
My relatives have turned against me
And find my conduct offensive
I have no one to call my own
But thee.
My boat has shuddered[116a] in mid-sea
And is now at a standstill.
No peace by day, no sleep by night.
I stand ever in expectation,
And am withering away.
The arrow of "absence" has pierced my heart,
And I cannot forget Thee for a moment.
You saved Ahalyā, turned to stone,
When you found her in the woods.
Is it such a burden to raise Mīrā,
Scarcely a tenth of her weight?[117]

119

Come to my house, stranger!
Bodily pain will go, joy will dawn.
Let us sing hymns together!
The peacock has heard the thunder
And is dancing in ecstasy!
Come to my courtyard now!
The lotus expands
When it beholds the moon,

And great will be my joy, too,
When I can see Thee.[118]
O my companion, I will feel cool
To the very pores of my skin.
Come to my courtyard, Mohan.
O Support of Thy Bhaktas,
Do not neglect Thy promise to me,
Mīrā is desolate, O courtly Giridhara!
Come to her,
And end her strife and pain.

120

Come to my house and talk to me,
O Shyām.
I shall be filled with joy and vigour,
And will offer myself, mind and body.
I am Thy loyal servant,
Pray do not forget it.
The sky emits thunder
And the clouds bring rain.
On hearing the cuckoo's call
The abandoned one, too,
Cries out for her lover.
Come to my house, Shyām,
I remain ever attached to Thy feet.
Take Mīrā into Thy protection.
She offers herself as a sacrifice,
Accept her as such.[119]

Rays of Hope

121

Today I heard to my great delight
That Hari had come.
Seeing that He has in fact not come,
I gaze down the road with yearning.
My eyes will not obey my commands

And emit a constant flow of tears.
What can I do?
I am at a perfect loss.
I have not wings to fly.
Says Mīrā: O my Master, the courtly Giridhara,
I await Your coming in great expectation.

122

The rainy season is abroad
And the skirt of my dress is wet.
You have gone off to distant lands,
And my heart finds it unbearable.
I keep sending letters to my Beloved
Asking when He will return.
Mīrā's Lord is the courtly Giridhara:
O Krishna, O Brother of Balrām,
Grant me Thy sight.

123

I send letters to my Beloved,
The dear Krishna.
But He sends no message of reply,
Purposely preserving silence.
I sweep His path in readiness
And gaze and gaze
Till my eyes turn blood-shot.
I have no peace by night or day,
My heart is fit to break.
O my Master, You were my companion
In former births.
When will You come?

124

Come to my house, O beautiful Shyām.
Without You I have no joy,
And have turned yellow as an autumn leaf.
I place faith in nothing else,
O my Master,

Except in contemplation of Thee.
May the Lord of Mīrā come quickly
And spare her further shame.

125

O Govind, for a loving friend,
Thy ways are devious indeed.[120]
I stand waiting for Him at the door,
And sweep the path
And thus my mind gains peace.
Only Thou knowest my heart,
And hence I breathe freely.
Mīrā's Lord is Hari, the Indestructible,
Whom she loved in a former birth.
Come, my Beloved,
In Thy absence I can no longer sleep.
I am gazing down Thy path.
Come, lovely Shyām, the Indestructible,
I enjoy no comfort,
And my heart is sorely distressed.
For Thy sake have I given up all.
Food and drink do not please me.
O Lord of Mīrā, Mīrā begs for darshan.
Hear her prayer.

127

O Gopāl,
Now I have developed true love
For Thy holy feet.
When my love began,
No one knew of it,
But now it is an open secret.[121]
Show compassion and grant me Thy sight,
Think of Thy servant this instant.
Says Mīrā, O my Lord,
O courtly Giridhara,
I offer myself wholly at Thy lotus feet.

128

My love has gone to those holy feet.
Without Thy sight, nothing pleases.
The world is a deceit and a delusion,
Or simply a dream.
My fear of the ocean of transmigration,
And all my worldly relationships,
Have I cast at Hari's feet.
Mīrā says. O my Lord, my courtly Giridhara,
All my hopes lie in taking refuge with Thee.

129

O Krishna, grant unto my love
Its due reward.
You are for me an ocean of virtues,
Regard not my defects.
The people of the world rate me,
But my heart pays no attention.
Come and speak a sweet word to me
With Thine own lips.[122]
I have been Thy servant for many births,
Come to my courtyard, I beg Thee.
Says Mīrā: O my Lord, the courtly Giridhara,
Lead my raft to the further shore.

130

Come to meet me, my Proud One,
I have fallen in love
With Thy beauteous form.
Enquire my name. I am known
As she whom "absence" drove to madness.
I enjoy peace neither by day nor night,
Like a fish separated from water.
Without Thy sight I can enjoy nothing
And am dying in writhing agony.
Mīrā is the servant of Thy feet.
Hear her prayer, O Beneficent One !

The Lord

131

Who but Thee will take notice of me,
O Giridhara, Holder of the Mountain?[123]
Thy crown of peacock-plumes
And Thy yellow waist-band are most becoming.
Strange is the beauty of Thy large ear-rings.
O Murāri, Thou didst protect the modesty
Of the daughter of Drupad[124]
In the midst of the packed assembly.
Says Mīrā, O my Master, the courtly Giridhara,
I offer myself as a sacrifice at Thy feet.

132

O Hari! Hear my petition, my King.
I am a weak girl, my Lord,
Protect my reputation.
Wherever I go I am Thine.
Hari has become the ornament of my heart.
Assuming the body of a horse,
You slew the Daityas
And fulfilled the purposes of the gods.[125]
Mīrā has no other Lord but Thee,
Thou art the crest-jewel on my head.[126]

133

I have taken refuge in Thee, O Krishna,
Save me in any way Thou wilt.
I have returned fruitless
From visiting the sixty-eight places of pilgrimage,[127]
But my mind will not accept defeat.
O Murāri, harken when I tell Thee
That in this world
I have none to call my own.
Servant Mīrā places her faith in Krishna.
Release her from the snare called "the world".

134

O Giridhara, I have taken refuge in Thee.
Protect me, O Ocean of Mercy!
You saved the sinner Ajāmil,[128]
And the low-cast Sadanā.[129]
You saved the elephant when he was drowning,[130]
You mounted the courtesan on a chariot.[131]
You have saved many other low creatures,
As the holy men relate. O Giridhara,
You saved the wild woman of the woods
And also the hunch-back woman,[132]
As all the world knows.
Thy virtues are past all telling,
Even the Vedas and Purāṇas are taxed.
Says Mīrā: Lord, my refuge is in Thee,
Harken to my prayer.

135

My Lord, I am offering a petition:
Take my raft to the further shore.
I have suffered much in this world,
Remove my doubts and afflictions.
The eight worldly pre-occupations[133]
Have set in: Oh, remove my pain.
The world is a flowing stream
Comprising eighty-four lakhs of births.
Mīrā's Lord is the courtly Giridhara.
May He end this coming and going
Once and for all.

136

O Storehouse of Compassion,
Lend Your ear to my prayer.
I love the holy hymns proclaiming Your glory,
But my life-breath ails.
I have no true relative or friend,
The whole world has turned against me.[134]

You saved the elephant bitten by a crocodile,
Redeeming Your pledge.
Servant Mīrā makes humble petition
That she has no other support but Thee.

137

Hari, I have heard that You save sinners,
And rescue them from the miseries
Of worldly existence.
You came running when You heard the cry
Of the drowning elephant.[135]
You remove the afflictions of Your devotees.
You lengthened the dress
Of the daughter of Drupad,
Humbling the pride of Duhshāsan.[136]
You kept Your promise to Prahlād,
Tearing open the belly of Hiraṇyakashipu.[137]
The wife of the rishi[138] received Your grace.
You removed the sufferings
Of the Brahmin Sudāmā.[139]
Says Mīrā: My Lord,
You know my request.
Why delay any further?

138

Shyām, now You have taken my arm!
Drowning in the ocean of transmigration,
I have taken refuge in You.
My defects are innumerable,
Who but You could tolerate me?
Says Mīrā: O my Lord, Hari the Indestructible,
Do not allow Your reputation[140] to falter.

139

O Shyām, O Govind, do not depart
From the orbit of my sight.
You sent the ox to the house of Kabīr,[140]
You mended Nām Dev's roof,[141]

You sowed Your servant Dhannā's field,[142]
You heard the elephant's cry.[143]
You ate the forest-woman's plums[144]
And Sudāmā's handful of rice.[145]
You accepted Karamā Bāī's dish,[146]
And took it with joy.
Shyām shines forth amidst a thousand Gopīs
Like the moon amidst the stars.
You fulfilled the needs of all Your saints,
But from Mīrā You remain aloof.

140

O my Beloved, I have felt the attraction
Of the holy Name. I have heard
That those who take the Name are saved,
The whole rock-hard world melts to water.[147]
I have earned no merit
And have amassed much demerit through sin.
The courtesan who taught her parrot
To repeat the holy Name
Was transported to the heaven of Vishnu.
The elephant only half-pronounced Your Name,
Yet all his troubles came to an end.
Descending from Garuḍa, You came running on foot,
And all his re-birth in animal wombs
Came to an end.
You exempted Ajāmil[148] from his sins
And his fear of death melted away.
He sang the holy Name
Simply by calling for his son,
This the whole world knows.[149]
You recognize faith when you see it,
And grant boons to those who seek refuge
With a pure heart.
Mīrā is Your servant,
Accept her as Your own!

Faith

141

Now my faith is strong,
Weak woman though I be.
The beautiful Shyām has come to my house.
I already have Hari for my necklace,
I will have Him for my ear-rings too,
Him, my bride-groom, Viṭṭhal Nāth.[150]
My crest-jewel is the Four-Armed Vishnu,
Whose image revolves in my mind—[151]
I need not go to a goldsmith.
My anklets are composed
Of Him who is the Life of the Universe.
Krishna is my arm-band,
And my foot-band too.
My foot-rings and dancer's anklets
Are Rāma Nārāyaṇa,[152]
The ring on my big toe, the Inner Ruler.[153]
I will have a casket affixed to my belt,
Made from the Supreme Spirit,[154]
A lock from the Name of Trivikram,[155]
A key from Him whose Joy is compassion.
There will I keep my treasures safe.
Now I am seated in the bride-groom's house,
Arrayed in finery and quite without shame.[156]
Says Mīrā: O my Master, the courtly Giridhara,
Henceforth I will address my petitions
To the feet of Hari.

142

Shrī Krishna has entered my heart
And the clouds have filled the sky.
Thunder roars, clouds quake
And the flashes of lightning inspire terror.
Cloud-banks mount as the east wind blows.
Frogs croak, the cuckoo sings,
And the cry of the peacock is heard.

Says Mīrā: O my Master, the courtly Giridhara,
My mind has gone to Thy lotus feet.

Expectation

143

I have heard that today Hari will come.
O my companion,
I will climb my high palace
To see when my King will come.
Frogs, peacocks and papīhās are calling,
The koil is striking its plaintive note.
Indra[157] is exulting, rain is falling everywhere,
The lightning is dancing without shame.
The earth robes herself anew
To greet Indra.
Says Mīrā; O my Master, the courtly Giridhara!
Come quickly, my King.

Meeting the Beloved

144

I offer a thousand thanks
To the astrologer who predicted Shyām would come.
My joy is overflowing, my soul has access
To an incalculable storehouse of joy.
I meet with my companions[158]
To honour and please the Beloved,
And there is joy all round.
O My dear companion,
Now that I have seen the Lord,
All my desires are fulfilled
And my sufferings forgotten.
Shyām, the Ocean of Joy, Mīrā's Lord,
Has entered her home.

145

O Shyām, today I have observed
The colourful ceremony of Gaurī Pūjā.[159]
Lightning flashes in black and coppery clouds
As the storm collects.
Frogs, peacocks and cuckoos are in full voice,
The koil is singing loudly.
Mīrā's Lord is the courtly Giridhara,
She stakes all on His holy feet.

146

Here are the clouds of the rainy season,
The rainy season so dear to the heart.
My heart overflows with delight
This rainy season,
As I have heard that Hari will come.
Thick and threatening clouds have collected,
The lightning brings with it steady rain.
Now the lightning is accompanied by light drops
And a delightful cool breeze.
Mīrā's Lord is the courtly Giridhara.
This is the time for auspicious hymns.

147

Come to my house, my Shyām,
For the rainy season fills me with emotion.
The clouds have collected from all quarters
And the thunder is roaring.
Frogs, peacocks and cuckoos cry out,
And the koil sings lustily.
Mīrā's Lord is the courtly Giridhara:
What she can offer is small.

148

Myself dyed deep with love and emotion,
I am playing Holī[160] with Shyām.
The red powder is flying,

The very clouds are red in the sky.
I am pumping out jets of coloured water
With the help of a squirt.
My pot is full of saffron
And various fragrant unguents.
Mīrā is the servant of the courtly Giridhara,
She is lying, handmaid, at His feet.

149

Come cloud, fill Thyself with water and come.
O my companion,
The raindrops are falling,
Just listen to the koil's cry.
A sweet breeze is playing
To the music of thunder,
And the sky is overcast with clouds.
Today the Beloved will come to my house.
I have prepared a bed for Him,
And you, O my companions,
Will sing Him songs of welcome.
Says Mīrā: O Hari, O Indestructible One,
Fortunate indeed are those who attain Thy side.

150

The Beloved has come to my house.
After many an age of expectation,
The abandoned one has found her Lover.
I am offering Him jewels as a present
And performing the Ārtī in His honour.
The Beloved is compassionate
And sent me a message.
My darkling Beloved has come,
Every limb in my body throbs with joy.[161]
My love is for that ocean of love, Hari.
His love has entrapped my eyes.
Says Mīrā: He is joy abundant,
I have enthroned Him on my brow

151

Come to my pavilion, O my King.
I have spread a bed
Made of delicately selected buds and blossoms,
And have arrayed myself in bridal garb
From head to toe.
I have been Thy slave during many births,
Thou art the be-all of my existence.[162]
Mīrā's Lord is Hari, the Indestructible.
Come, grant me Thy sight at once.

152

I am deeply attached to Thy beauty,
O Lover of Rādhā, O Great King.
Robed in saffron,
He wears a jewel-studded crown
With a peacock plume.
With His alligator-earrings
And peacock-plume crown
He is the very picture of refinement.[163]
Mīrā's Lord is the courtly Giridhara.
She says: Today I have met my King.

Self-Dedication

153

Go to the place where the Beloved abides,
Go to the place where you may find Him.
If the Beloved tells me,
I will put on a red sārī,
If he tells me,
I will don the ochre robe.
I will decorate my hair-parting with pearls
Or leave my scattered locks unkempt,
Either according to His wish.
Mīrā's Lord is the courtly Giridhara.
She says: Harken to the praises of my King.

154

O Giridhara Lāl, keep me as Thy servant.
Keep me as Thy servant.
I will remain Thy faithful servant,
Will plant Thy garden,
And every morning will rise early
To have Thy sight.
In the leafy lanes of Brindāvan
I will sing the deeds of Govind.
If I perform Thy service,
I will have Thy sight for reward.
Thy remembrance will be my wages,
The spirit of devotion my fief,
For which I have longed during many a birth.
Beautiful is Krishna with His peacock crown,
His Yellow waist-cloth
And His glittering necklace of gems.
Mohan, the flute-player,
Is grazing the cows in Brindāvan.
I will make fresh green bowers for Him,
With borders between.
Robed in a scarlet sārī,
I shall enjoy the sight of Shyām,
Mīrā's Lord is the courtly Giridhara,
Her heart is in much perturbation.
I request to have sight of the Lord
At midnight by the banks of the Yamunā.

155

O my companion,
Shyām shot an arrow
That has pierced me through.
The fire of longing
Is burning in my heart
And my whole body is in torment.
My roving mind cannot stir,
Fettered in the chains of love.
No one but myself and my Beloved

Knows the extent of my pain.[164]
I can do nothing, my companion,
But weep copious tears.
Mīrā says, "My Lord, unless you come
My life cannot endure."

The World

156

O my companion,
Without Shyām I suffer greatly. Without Him,
Who can give me strength to endure?
The world is a hissing cauldron of error.
It takes no joy
In cultivating the society of the good.
They abuse the holy men
While themselves earning demerit
By their wicked deeds.
Without the Name of God
One does not gain liberation,
One merely circulates
In the eighty-four lakhs of wombs.
The fools waste their precious lives,
Not seeking the society of the good
Even in a dream.
Mīrā says: My Lord, I take refuge in Thee.
Thus will I attain
The highest state open to man.

157

The people of the world
Would die of shame
To be caught taking the Name of God.
They will tramp round the whole village,
But feel too fatigued
To visit the temple of Hari.

If a quarrel arises
They run to it at once,
Leaving what they are doing in the house.
To hear a buffoon crack jests,
Or to watch a courtesan dance,
They will sit twelve hours at a stretch
Mīrā's Lord is the courtly Giridhara.
She has taken refuge at His lotus feet.

158

You cannot call this true devotion,
To bathe one's forehead and apply the tilak
Without cleansing the impurities of the heart.
That cruel cur desire
Has bound me with the cord of greed.
The butcher of anger remains within me,
How can I hope to meet Gopāl?
The greedy senses are like a cat,
And I keep on giving them food.
Weakened by my hunger for sense-objects
I do not take the Name of God.
I worship not God but myself,
And glow with ecstasy.
Now that I have built up
This towering rock of pride,
Where can the water of true wisdom collect?[165]
You cannot deceive Him who knows
The inmost recesses of your soul.
The Name of Hari does not enter my heart,
Though I tell with my lips
The beads of my bejewelled rosary.
Learn to love the compassionate Lord,
Give up faith in the world.
Mīrā is the slave of the courtly Giridhara,
She has adopted the path of simple detachment.[166]

159

How can one come to meet the Lord?
For fifteen hours one is busy,

And the remaining nine one sleeps.
Having received the priceless gift
Of a human birth,
We remain asleep and it is wasted.
Mīrā's Lord is the courtly Giridhara.
She says: What is to be must be,
Worship the Lord.

The Land of Braj

160

O my companion, the sight of Brindāvan
Has become very dear to me.
In every house the Lord is worshipped
By the offering of tulsi-leaves,
And they enjoy the sight of the Lord
With reverence.
The pure water of the Yamunā flows,
And their sole nourishment is milk and curds.
The Lord sits on a gem-studded throne,
Wearing a crown of tulsi-leaves.
O Shyām, I walked[167] from bower to bower,
Listening to the sounds of Thy flute.
Mīrā's Lord is the courtly Giridhara,
She says, "Without worship of the Lord,
Man is a feeble creature."

161

O my mind,
Let us go to the bank of the Yamunā.
My whole body has been refreshed
By the pure waters of the Yamunā.
Krishna was playing His flute
In the company of Balvir.[168]
His peacock's feather crown
And yellow loincloth are charming.
The diamonds in His ear-rings sparkle.

Mīrā's Lord is the courtly Giridhara—
Behold, He is playing with Balvīr.

The Childish Sports

162

O Krishna, who braided Thy jet-black locks?
Was it Yashodā who prepared Thy toilet
With such a dexterous hand
And such bewitching art?
If You once come into my little house
I will shut its sandalwood doors
And pull the bolt.
Mīrā's Lord is the courtly Giridhara.
She offers herself in sacrifice
To those beautiful locks.

163

Welcome, O Dweller in Gokul!
The women of Gokul are ravished
At Thy sight.
Some sing, some dance, some laugh.
The Lord has donned a yellow loincloth
And is fragrant with the scent of aloes.
To such a handsome Master as Giridhara,
One like Mīrā will be a slave,

164

O my companion, my Krishna,
Has veritably become a fragment of my heart.
Lovely are His peacock-plume crown,
His yellow loincloth and rippling ear-rings.
The Son of Nand is busy dancing
In the bowers and lanes of Brindāban.
Mīrā's Lord is the courtly Giridhara:
She has taken refuge at the lotus feet
Of that Stealer of the Heart.

165

Wake up, my dear flute player,
Wake up, my darling.
The night has passed,
Dawn has come,
People are opening their doors.
You can hear the gopīs churning the curds,
Harken to the clink of their bracelets.
Wake up, Lāl jī, the dawn has come,
Men and gods alike
Are waiting at Thy door to greet Thee.
The cowherd boys are in a frenzy,
Everywhere there are shouts of "Jai! Jai!"
Now the little herdsmen
Have taken their parcels of bread and butter
Ready to go out.
Mīrā's Lord is the courtly Giridhara.
He saves those
Who choose Him for their refuge.

The Playing of The Flute

166

On the banks of the Yamunā
The flute was heard.
The Flute-Player has captured my heart,
My soul has not strength to withstand.
Dark Himself,
Krishna is seated on a dark blanket
By the dark waters of the Yamunā.
On hearing the sounds of the flute
I lose body-consciousness,
My body remaining like a stone.
Says Mīrā, O my Lord,
The courtly Giridhara,
Come quickly and end my pain.

167

Sister, the sound of the flute
Has driven me crazy.
Without Hari, nothing avails.
On hearing the sounds
I loose body-consciousness,
My heart well caught
In the meshes of the net.
What vows and observances have you performed,
O flute? Who is now at your side?
The magic of those seven notes
Has entrapped even Mīrā's Lord Himself.

The Serpent

168

O Thou of the lotus-leaf eyes,
Thou didst tame the black serpent.[169]
Thou didst subdue the serpent
In a pool of the Yamunā,
Dancing on his ruffled black crests.
Thou didst leap into the water without fear.
For Thou art one,
But Thy powers are infinite.
Mīrā's Lord, the courtly Giridhara,
Is the darling of the women of Braj.

Stealing The Clothes

169

Sister, today that little monkey
Stole my sārī and sat with it
On the branch of a Kadamba tree.[170]
Sister, today that little monkey Giridhara
Met me on the road.

I had gone to the Yamunā
To fetch water,
When along came Krishna Murāri.
The little monkey stole my sārī,
And I was left standing naked
In the water.
My companions all laughed
And clapped their hands to see my plight.[171]
My mother-in law is ill-natured,
My sister-in-law morose,
They quarrel with me and abuse me.
Mīrā's Lord is the courtly Giridhara.
She offers herself in sacrifice
To His lotus feet.

170

Murāri gave my sārī a twitch.
The pot of dye I was carrying
Fell from my head.
My nose-ring slipped off
And got caught in my sārī.
My hair broke loose
And became entangled in my ear-rings,
The tip of my sārī was torn.
The Charmer of Hearts was in wanton mood,
That delicate exponent of the art of love.
Mīrā's Lord is the courtly Giridhara,
She places her head at His lotus feet.[172]

The Tryst

171

Giridhara is coming down my lane,
And I have hidden myself for shame.
A brilliant red turban,
A yellow dress,
And a chaplet of flowers [173] covering it :

A parasol arches over His crown,
And the beauty of His ear-rings
Passes description.
I[174] will wear a yellow satin skirt
With a rich bodice above.
Seeing Krishna Murāri coming,
His dear Rādhā has hidden.
She wears a lovely peacock-plume crown,
Her nose-ring is charming,
And a glittering necklace of pearls
Hangs from her neck.
I offer myself in sacrifice
To her lotus feet.
Darling Rādhā stands in supplication,
Saying, "O Krishna Murāri,
Hear my prayer."
Mīrā's Lord is the courtly Giridhara,
She offers herself in sacrifice
To His lotus feet.

The Steps to The River

172

O my companion,
My Mohan has stolen my heart.
What shall I do?
Where shall I go?
My life-breaths are wedded to the Lord
In total dedication.
O my companion,
I was going to fetch water
With my water-pot balanced on my head.
Suddenly a dark form,
Not yet grown to full manhood,
Appeared before me
And bound me in His spell.
I caste off worldly shame

And thus my cause prospered.
Mīrā is the slave of Lāl Giridhara:
She chose her bridegroom carefully.

173

The dagger of love has pierced my heart.
I was going to the river to fetch water,
A golden pitcher[175] on my head.
Hari jī has bound me
By the thin thread of love,
And wherever He draws me,
Thither I go.
Mīrā's Lord is the courtly Giridhara:
This is the nature
Of His dark and beautiful form.

174

O my companion,
The sight of Shyām is like a dagger.
I have lost body-consciousness[176]
And am reduced to a ruinous state.
My body is pervaded by pain,
My heart in a state of intoxication.
Three or four companions are with me,
All in a state of madness.
I know Him well,
He is the "Stroller in the Woods"
The partridge longs only for the moon,
The lamp burns the moth,
The fish dies without water.
This is the love that is precious.
If I do not see Him
How can I live?
My heart finds peace nowhere.
Go to Krishna
And tell Him that Mīrā is His.

Holī

175

Giridhara is playing Holī
He plays to perfection
The flute, the lute and the drums,
Along with his companions, the women of Braj.
Mohan Bihārī scatters with His own hand
The sandalwood and saffron.
In large handfuls He flings the red powder
In all directions
And it falls on everyone.
There is the handsome youth Krishna,
And with Him is Rādhā,
Dear to Him as His life.
He sings the apprporiate songs for Holī,
Clapping exquisitely in time with the music.
That great artist Shyām is playing Holī,
And all Braj is flooded with joy.
Mīrā's Lord is the courtly Giridhara,
Is Mohan Lāl, "The Stroller in the Woods".

Selling The Curds

176

Where are You taking me, Krishna?
In the lanes and bowers of Brindāban,
He has taken me by the hand.
He ate my curds and broke the pot
And took me in His arms.
He jumped at me,
And dashed my pot to the ground,
That dark figure with the beautiful limbs.
O Mohan,
You came and went freely in Gokul,
But would never accept my curds.

Mīrā's Lord is the courtly Giridhara,
Her Master from birth to birth.

177

O my companion,
What I saw in Braj today was magic.
A Gopī [177] was carrying a pot
When she found herself confronted
By the Son of Nand.
O my companion,
She forgot the word for curds outright
And just said
"Will someone take the beautiful Shyām?"
In the leafy lane of Brindāvan,
The Charmer of Hearts
Fixed His glance on the maiden and left.
Mīrā's Lord is the courtly Giridhara,
The beautiful, handsome, savorous Shyām.

178

She is wandering about, pot on head,
Saying "Who will take the beautiful Shyām?"
The Gopī has forgotten the word for curds,
And is saying "Take Hari, take Hari."
Mīrā's Lord is the courtly Giridhara,
She has accepted slavery without payment.
The Gopī is dazzled by Krishna's beauty,
And is babbling aimlessly.

The Departure For Mathurā

179

O Hari, where have You gone
After coming and sowing the seeds of love?
You sowed the seeds of love,
And stole my heart,

And drew forth a piteous cry.
I believe I will take poison and die.
You set the boat of love in motion
And abandoned it in midstream.
You betrayed me and left me.
O Lord of Mīrā,
You are dallying in Mathurā,
When will You come?

180

Shyām has disappeared from view
Like the fragile moon.[178]
Having gone to Mathurā
He has become a citizen of that city,
But us He has caught
In the noose of love.
Mīrā's Lord is the courtly Giridhara,
It seems that now His love is waning.

181

Shyām has stalked off to punish me
And is frolicking about with other women.
He will not even speak to me.
He will not even come into my lane,
But steps into the courtyards of others.
He will not even touch my finger,
But twists the arms of others.
He will not touch my shawl,
But He lifts the veil of others.
Shyām is Mīrā's Lord,
But He wanders about like a rake.

182

O my companion,
My modesty was my enemy.
Why did I not go off
With Shrī Lāl Gopāl?

The cruel Akrūr[179] came in a decorated chariot.
He seated Gopāl on the chariot
And drove off,
Leaving me wringing my hands.
My heart must be of steel
Not to break. Shyām left me,
And now my whole body
Is burning with the pain of longing.
Mīrā is the slave of Lāl Giridhara,
Why is she not already dead and scattered?

Conversation With Uddhava

183

O Uddhava,[180] it is all the fault
Of our own Karma:
It is useless to blame others.
O Harken, my companions,
It was while walking on the path
That I suffered the blow.
At first I did not understand,[181]
I had chosen the road of[182] egoism.
I did not think Hari would leave me,
But our good and evil fortune
Is written by the finger of fate.
Mīrā's Lord is Hari, the Indestructible.
Come, Lord, remove her pain.

184

The impulse comes into my mind
To rove about in company with Gopāl.
When I beheld the beauty
Of His lotus face
I lost control of my faculties.
Let me take flute and staff in hand
And don a yellow loin-cloth.
Let me rove about with the herds,

Clad like a herdsman
And wearing a peacock-plume crown.
See, I have become a lovely creeper
Gracing the Brindāban nights.[183]
I see the beasts and birds and monkeys
And hear the discourses of the sages.
The elders have laid down
A narrow code of conventional behaviour.
To whom can I open my heart?
O Mīrā, find the Lord Giridhara
And continue your life like this.

185

O Uddhav, who will read this letter
In the absence of the Lord,
Who will read it?[184]
You came with this piece of paper,
But where did you leave your Comrade?
Our feet are worn with walking
And our eyes have turned bloodshot.
Rādhā took the letter
And sat reading it.
Her heart overflowed.
Water streamed from her lotus eyes
Like the mighty flow of the Ganges.
She turned yellow like an autumn leaf,
And would not touch food.
In the absence of Hari,
Her heart was burning
Like the wick of a lamp.
My faith is in Krishna[185]
Who saved the drowning elephant.
Mīrā is the slave of Lāl Giridhara,
Her companion on a narrow path.

The Wild Woman of the Woods

186

The wild woman of the woods[186]
Found out the sweet plums by tasting them
And brought them to the Lord.
She was neither civilized nor educated
Nor possessed of physical beauty.
She was of low caste and filthy apparel,
But the Lord accepted her soiled plums,
Knowing the sincerity of her love.
She recognized no distinctions of high and low,
But sought only the pure milk of love.
Not for her the learning of the Veda,
She was transported to heaven on a chariot
At a single stroke.
Now she sports in Vaikunth,[187]
Bound to Hari by ties of love.
Says servant Mīrā:
Whoso loves like this is saved.
The Lord is the Saviour of the Fallen
And I was a cowherd-maiden at Gokul
In a former birth.

Sudāmā

187

The Lord smiled to see Sudāmā,[189]
The Lord smiled.
His shoes worn to shreds,
He came unshod,
His feet blistering on the way.
"You were my childhood friend, Sudāmā,
Why do you now live so far?
Has Bhābhī[190] sent Me a present?"
Yes, the present consisted

Of a handful and a half of rice.
On arriving back home,
Sudāmā exclaimed in surprise:
"My Lord,
Where has my broken-down cottage gone?
What is this palace,
Studded with diamonds, rubies and pearls?
Where are my cow and calf?
What mean these elephants
Chained by the doorway?
Mīrā's Lord is Hari, the Indestructible.
She says: I have taken sanctuary with Thee.

Reaping The Fruits of one's Deeds

188

O Jogī, I did not plumb Thy depths.
I[191] took up my āsan
And sat in a cave:
I engaged in contemplation of Hari,
Beads round my neck,
Cloth[192] in hand, body covered in ashes.
Mīrā's Lord is Hari, the Indestructible.
What was written in her fate,[193]
That she received.

189

Nothing can halt the course of Karma.
King Harishchandra the Truthful[194]
Carried water in the house of the sweeper.
The bones of Draupadī,
Queen of the Five Pāṇḍus,
Rotted on the Himālayan slopes.[195]
Bali performed a sacrifice
Aimed at taking him to Indra's throne,
But ended up in the nether regions.[195a]

Mīrā's Lord is the courtly Giridhara.
He changed the poison to nectar.[196]

190

Strange are the decrees of fate.
Behold the large eyes of the deer!
Yet he is forced to roam the forests.
The harsh crane has brilliant plumage,
While the sweet-voiced cuckoo is black.
The rivers flow in pure streams,
But the sea makes them salt.
Fools sit on thrones as kings,
While the wise beg their bread.
Mīrā's Lord is the courtly Giridhara:
The King persecutes the Bhaktas.[196a]

191

Do not mention the name of love,
O my simple-minded companion.
Strange is the path
When you offer your love.
Your body is crushed at the first step.
If you want to offer love
Be prepared to cut off your head
And sit on it.
Be like the moth,
Which circles the lamp and offers its body.
Be like the deer, which, on hearing the horn,
Offers its head to the hunter.
Be like the partridge,
Which swallows burning coals
In love of the moon.[197]
Be like the fish,
Which yields up its life
When separated from the sea.
Be like the bee,

Entrapped in the closing petals of the lotus.
Mīrā's Lord is the courtly Giridhara
She says: Offer your mind
To those lotus feet.

192

Only he knows the bitterness of love
Who has deeply felt its pangs.
When you are in trouble
No one comes near you:
When fortune smiles,
All come to share the joy.
Love shows no external wound,
But the pain pervades every pore
Devotee Mīrā offers her body
As a sacrifice to Giridhara for ever.

193

Go to that impenetrable realm
That Death himself trembles to look upon.
There plays the fountain of love
With swans sporting on its waters.[197a]
There the company of holy men is available,
And one may talk of spiritual knowledge.[198]
There one can meditate on Shyām
And purify one's mind.
There one may bind on
The anklets of good-conduct,
And dance the dance of inner contentment.
There one may adopt a headpiece of gold
And the sixteen kinds of adornment.[199]
Let there be love for Shyām
And indifference to all else.

Spiritual Teaching

194

That dark Dweller in Braj
Is my only refuge.
O my companion,
Worldly comfort is an illusion,
As soon you get it, it goes.
I have chosen the Indestructible for my refuge,
Him whom the snake of death
Will not devour.
My Beloved dwells in my heart,
I have actually seen that Abode of Joy.
Mīrā's Lord is Hari, the Indestructible.
My Lord, I have taken refuge with Thee,
Thy slave.

195

O my mind,
Worship the lotus feet of the Indestructible One!
Whatever thou seest twixt earth and sky
Will perish.
Why undertake fasts and pilgrimages?
Why engage in philosophical discussions?
Why commit suicide in Banāras?
Take no pride in the body,
It will soon be mingling with the dust.
This life is like the sporting of sparrows,
It will end with the onset of night.
Why don the ochre robe
And leave home as a sannyāsī?
Those who adopt the external garb of a Jogī,
But do not penetrate to the secret,
Are caught again in the net of rebirth.
Mīrā's Lord is the courtly Giridhara.
Deign to sever, O Master,
All the knots in her heart.

196

We do not get a human life
Just for the asking.
Birth in a human body
Is the reward for good deeds
In former births.
Life waxes and wanes imperceptibly,
It does not stay long.
The leaf that has once fallen
Does not return to the branch.
Behold the Ocean of Transmigration,
With its swift, irresistible tide.
O Lāl Giridhara, O pilot of my soul,
Swiftly conduct my barque to the further shore.
Mīrā is the slave of Lāl Giridhara.
She says: Life lasts but a few days only.

197

Life in the world is short,
Why shoulder an unnecessary load
Of worldly relationships?
Thy parents gave thee birth in the world,
But the Lord ordained thy fate.
Life passes in getting and spending,
No merit is earned by virtuous deeds.
I will sing the praises of Hari
In the company of holy men,
Nothing else concerns me.
Mīrā's Lord is the courtly Giridhara,
She says: Only by Thy power
Have I crossed to the further shore.

198

Do not forget thy duty to serve,
O servant.
Thy joys are of short duration,

Like the blossom on the pomegranate.
You came here for the sake of profit,
But forgot your capital
And threw it away.
Mīrā's Lord is the courtly Giridhara.
She says:
In this world you must practise detachment.

199

O my mind,
Drink the nectar of the Name of God.[200]
Drink the nectar of the Name of God.
Give up evil company,
And continually keep the company
Of holy men.
Listen to the accounts of Hari
That proceed from their lips.
Expel lust, anger, pride, greed and infatuation
From thy mind.
Mīrā's Lord is the courtly Giridhara,
She is soaked in His love.[201]

200

O my mind,
I repeat continually the Name of Shyām.
O ye living creatures,
Through repeating the Name of Shyām
I have absolved a million sins.
The Name of Shyām has destroyed
Ancient sins of many a former birth.
It is a draft of nectar
In a golden cup,
Who could refuse to drink it?
Mīrā's Lord is Hari, the Indestructible.
She is dissolved in Shyām,
Body and mind.

201

My love for Shyām has set in,
And my eyes have known
The joy of His sight.
O my companion,
I arrayed myself in full adornment,
And the Beloved came running to meet me.
I have chosen no miserable bridegroom
Who will die at each rebirth.
O my companion,
I have chosen Shyām for my bridegroom,
Who will be my crest-jewel immortal.
Krishna has requited my love,
That has lasted from birth to birth.
Mīrā says, O Hari! O Indestructible One!
When will you come to my side?

202

Ranachor[202] has stolen my heart.
His peacock-plume crown
Waves over His head like a royal parasol,
The beauty of His ear-rings
Outreaches description.
The sea is washing His feet,
While the Gomatī River flows on nearby.
Flags on poles adorn its banks,
Festooned with swaying strings of pearls.[203]
Our Lord and Master Ranachor
Ever provides for the welfare of His devotees.
Mīrā says: O my Master,
O courtly Giridhara, O Nand Kishor, [204]
Deign to grasp me by the hand.

NOTES

1
Pain arising from the inevitable diseases of the body, pain due to the work of malignant divine or demoniac forces, and pain arising from the interplay of the elements, for example the pain arising from drought or flood.

2
Prahlāda was the son of Hiraṇyakaśipu, king of the demons. Persecuted by his father, Prahlāda remained constant in devotion to Viṣṇu. One day his father asked him, "Where is your God ?" Prahlāda replied, "He is everywhere, even in this pillar." Hiraṇyakaśipu kicked the pillar with his foot, whereupon the Lord sprang out from it in the form of a "Man-Lion" and destroyed him. Eventually the Lord elevated Prahlāda to the rank of Indra, whose place as king of the gods had been usurped by the demon Hiraṇyakaśipu.

3
Dhruva performed austerities at the command of his mother while yet a child, and was eventually granted the following boon : "Thou shalt attain to fixity above all the worlds, planets and constellations, and shalt exist as their support. Thy place of abode will be called Dhruva-loka." This world manifests to us as the pole-star.

4
The demon Bali threatened to conquer and tyrannize over the universe, but the Lord appeared in the form of a dwarf (Vāman) and asked to be given as much land as He could bestride in three paces. Granted the boon, He caused His body to swell in size till all heaven and earth were covered in two strides. The third stride confined Bali's powers to the infernal regions.

5
Ahalyā or Ahilyā, wife of the seer Gautama, was turned to stone by her husband's curse. But she was brought back to life by the touch of the foot of the Lord Viṣṇu in His incarnation as Rāma.

6
Kāliya was a five-headed serpent dwelling in a pool in the Jumna near Bṛndāvana, from which he would sally forth and cause great destruction. The child Kṛṣṇa placed His foot on the middle head of the serpent and forced him to leave Bṛndāvana for the sea.

7
When Kṛṣṇa diverted the cowherds of Bṛndāvana from worship of Indra, the god threatened to deluge them with rain. But Kṛṣṇa tore up the Govardhana hill near the village and held it aloft on His little finger to serve as an umbrella.

8

The name "Giridhara" by which Mīrābāī constantly addresses Kṛṣṇa means "He who held aloft the Mountain" and refers to the incident recorded in the previous note. Lāla is an affectionate term for a child. The Sanskrit form Giridhara has been preserved in the translation, though it appears that Mīrā regularly used the form Giradhara.

9

As long as the soul remains bereft of the grace of God, it continues to act with egoism and attachment, and such action forces it to return to earth in a new body to experience the "fruits" or moral deserts of that action. Thus the soul becomes involved in continual rebirth in new bodies, exposed to the certainty of suffering, disease and death. As this process is self-perpetuating and inevitable until the soul is rescued by the grace of the Lord, it is called an "unnavigable sea" and He the raft.

10

A name for Kṛṣṇa which means "He who enjoys the pleasures of gay company" and also "A stroller, a wanderer".

11

A small round mark of sandal-paste or other colouring matter placed between the eye-brows as an ornament or as an auspicious mark on ceremonial occasions.

12

The name of the district round Āgrā and Mathurā where Kṛṣṇa's exploits as a child took place.

13

A name of Kṛṣṇa meaning "The Charming One".

14

Kṛṣṇa was the son of Vasudeva, and was born in Mathurā. But he was hidden away in the neighbouring villages on the Jumna by his parents to thwart the murderous intentions of His wicked maternal uncle, King Kaṃsa of Mathurā. First He went to Gokula, and at the age of seven moved on to Bṛndāvana. He was brought up there by his foster-mother Yaśodā in the family of Nanda, the local tribal chief.

15

I.e. the Vijayantī Mālā of Viṣṇu, a necklace composed of five kinds of gems, viz. pearl, ruby, emerald, sapphire and diamond.

16

Literally "The Cowherd", and therefore referring to Kṛṣṇa in particular during His boyhood in Bṛndāvana. It is taught that Viṣṇu, the Lord God, made "descents" to earth ("Incarnations" or Avatāras), of which those as Rāma and Kṛṣṇa are the most important.

17

An affectionate name for the Lord God Viṣṇu, explained by the Bhaktas as meaning "He who steals away the sins of His devotees."

18

From Vedic times, the Hindus have believed in three planes of existence, manifested as (1) the earth together with the nether regions, (2) the space between the earth and the "roof" of the sky, and (3) an abode of perpetual light hidden beyond the roof of the sky. The deity presiding over these three worlds is invoked in the syllables "bhūr bhuvaḥ svaḥ" pronounced before the recitation of the sacred Gāyatrī verse.

19

No worldly object is worthy of complete love, because all are transient. But the Lord from whom objects proceed and into whom they ultimately dissolve is a worthy object of our supreme love because He is eternal and indestructible.

20

"Dweller in Braj", a name of Kṛṣṇa.

21

The "Nāgara" of "Giridhara Nāgara" means "a townsman" and hence "polished", "sophisticated" and "skilled in the arts of love". Students of the Śrīmad Bhāgavata will remember how sensitive the village girls of Braj were about Kṛṣṇa's association with the fine ladies of the court and town of Mathurā. "Nāgara" has been translated as "courtly" throughout.

22

"The Dark One", a name given to Kṛṣṇa in allusion to the dark colour of His body, the colour of a rain-cloud.

23

A design having magical properties.

24

A verbal spell.

25

Probably the "house" means "the body" and the meaning is "How can I continue to live ?" One of the alternative versions quoted by D. S. Bhāṭī has "body" instead of "house".

26

I.e. the "three-bended" pose, standing with legs crossed, body slightly bent from the waist and arms raised and curved to play the flute.

27

"The Intoxicator".

28

The old Sanskrit name "Yamunā" has been preserved to refer to the river Jumna, which flows down from Delhi past Bṛndāvana and Mathurā. But Mīrā herself uses the modern form.

29

"Enemy of the demon Mura", a name of Kṛṣṇa.

30

The words in the original are "Rāma jī". Opinions differ about Mīrā's use of the name Rāma. I follow Śaśi Prabhā in thinking that she used it basically as a name for Kṛṣṇa, as virtually all the imagery used in the present edition of the Padāvalī concerns Kṛṣṇa. When reference is made to acts of compassion traditionally attributed to Viṣṇu in His various forms and incarnations, they are attributed by Mīrā personally to Śyāma, Poem 139. Except at Poem 186, no scenes from the life of Rāma son of Daśaratha are depicted. Admittedly the word "Rāma" was used by the Sant poets, to whom Mīrā owes some degree of allegiance, quite generally in the sense of "God". But a particularly clear instance of the use of "Rāma" to mean "Kṛṣṇa" is recorded at Note 58, Poem 55.

31

See Note 16.

32

There are other versions of this famous poem in which the reference to miraculous delivery from the effects of poison does not occur, and one cannot but suspect that the line is an interpolation. If it is taken as genuine, it would have to be presumed that the whole poem was composed after Mīrā had left Mewār, and that the reference was to an attempt made on her life by Vikramājīta Siṃha, her borther-in-law. See the account of her life in the Introduction and Note 41 below.

33

The reference to a miraculous escape from a black serpent concealed in a basket is less well attested in the early hagiographical literature than the attempted poisoning. (Padmāvatī, p. 85) One must assume that if the poem is accepted as authentic, the line must be an interpolation.

33a

The mystics join hands down the ages and all across continents. Ācārya Caturvedī very appositely compares this poem with the "Man az 'ālam tu rā tanhā guzīnam" of Jalāl uddīn Rūmī, which is translated in R. A. Nicholson, "Dīvāni Shamsi Tabrīz", Cambridge 1898 (reprinted 1952) p. 121.

34

This is thought to be a reminiscence by Mīrā of her previous life associated with Śrī Kṛṣṇa as the Gopī Lalitā.

35

Reading karāṃrī.

36

Reading gail. The commentators differ over the reading and the meaning.

37

Cp. Note 34.

38

The body, composed of the five elements enumerated in classical Hindu physics — ether, wind, fire, water, earth.

39

Perhaps the world, perhaps Mīrā's royal home. The commentators differ over this obscure line.

40

Kṛṣṇa. From gopa+indra=Great Cowherd.

41

Many authorities have expressed doubts about the authenticity of the poems 30-42 and others which refer either to persecution by a king or to miraculous deliverances from attempts made by him on Mīrā's life. The earliest surviving biographical notice, that of the Bhakta-Māla of Nābhā Dāsa, mentions an unsuccessful attempt on Mīrā's life by poisoning. This seems credible enough, given the times in which she lived. But as there is a tradition in Dvāraka that Mīrā was successfully poisoned in Cittaur (Padmāvatī, p. 60), and as similar traditions are circulated about Godā, Mīrā's counterpart among the Tamil Ālvārs, one has to reckon with the possibility that even the earliest and simplest form of the tradition was no more than a rumour, eagerly accepted and spread to glorify the saint. The later biographical literature appears to build on this first account and embellish it. Fresh accounts of other escapes from death appear, in which the miraculous element is further accentuated. The poems that refer to these "events" are suspect in style as well as in content. (Padmāvatī, p. 85, p. 176 : Goetz, p. 42 : Caturvedī, p. 6, p. 22 : D. S. Bhāṭī, p. 237). For the context in which these poems are today usually understood when taken as genuine, see Note 32.

42

The reference is probably to sects who practised woman-worship in its cruder forms. Banārasī Prasāda Saksenā mentions the special connection of the Rājpūts with Śākta forms of worship at Dhīrendra Varmā, p. 37.

43

The word "jana" may here only mean "Hari jana", devotees of Hari, as in the last line of Poem 59. But the mention of a "narrow path" may imply that the reference is to the Guru. Kabīr speaks of the spiritual path as being "narrow" because there is not room for two on it. The pupil has to dissolve his individuality in that of the Guru.

44

The reference should be taken as being to King Vikramājīta. But see Notes 32 and 41.

45

I.e. I will leave it. Cp. Poem 39.

46

Reading thārī with D. S. Bhāṭī and Śaśi Prabhā.

47

Reading mhāṇe with Śaśi Prabhā, which eliminates the obviously questionable interpretation "māṃ ne". On Madan, see Note 27.

47a

According to the most widely accepted view, Queen Karmavatī, mother of Vikramājīta Siṃha.

48

Reading rākhi.

49

The feet of the image of the Lord would be ceremonially washed in Pūjā.

50

Śālagrāma is a black ammonite form of stone found by the Gaṇḍakī River, north of Patna. It is worshipped as the Lord Viṣṇu.

51
I.e. Mīrā herself.
52
Literally, "my nine-stringed necklace".
53
See Note 49.
54
The name Jogī suggests a wandering ascetic of the Nātha sect. As he is cut off from worldly attachments, he comes and goes like a passing cloud and nobody can get a hold on him.
55
Reading gāṃsī. By singing "piyu piyu" the cuckoo reminds Mīrā of her Beloved (priya, priyatama, pati).
56
It is related in the Eighth Skandha of the Śrīmad Bhāgavata, Chapters 2-4, how the Lord Viṣṇu came to the rescue of an elephant whose foot was caught by a river-monster when he was bathing in a pool. The story illustrates how the Lord will come immediately to the rescue of anyone, provided they recognize the futility of their own individual efforts and call on Him sincerely for help.

57
There appear to have been circular saws at Kāśī (Banāras) and Prayāga (Allahabad) and other holy places where lost souls could commit suicide in the hope of gaining spiritual merit.
58
The name Rāma is used, but it seems to be a clear case of the use of the name Rāma to mean Kṛṣṇa. Cp. Note 30.
59
Reading chāṃḍi with D. S. Bhāṭī and Śaśi Prabhā.
60
Eka-rasūṃ = eka-rasa hokara. (Śaśi Prabhā) But the interpretation given in the translation is admittedly speculative.
61
Charmer of the Heart, Kṛṣṇa.
62
The commentators differ over the meaning of the word "sadana", but "new-born" seems the more natural interpretation and can be supported from the Braja Bhāṣā Sūra Kośa. Thus I follow D.S. Bhāṭī.
63
Items of the wandering Jogī's equipment. The "selī" is a length of black wool wound round the Jogī's horn. H. P. Dvivedī, Kabīr, p. 28.
64
Naiṇ aṇiyāle. On this, cp. "naina kamala-dala se aniyāre" quoted from the Sūra Sāgara in the Braja Bhāṣā Sūra Kośa under the heading "aniyāre".
65
In the present translation "Ramāīyā" and its variants are translated

"Kṛṣṇa", in line with the suggestion at Note 30. The authorities do not agree on the meaning here. It has been explained as "Rāma"="God" in a general and unspecific sense, and also as the "All-Pervading One" and "He who dwells in every heart", and also in other ways.

66

Literally : "Do not eat milky rice-pudding." One moment it is so hot that it burns your tongue, the next it is cold and tasteless.

67

Reading "jhaṭak", and understanding the phrase as "jhaṭak apnā nāśa batātā hai."

68

In this poem, Mīrā seems to be reflecting on the difficulties of spiritual love. First she reflects that to His devotees the Lord appears like a tease, first granting His love and then withdrawing it. Then she seems to reflect despairingly on her insufficiencies, on the disparity between herself and her Lord and on her own presumption. Finally the despair melts away with the dawning of an ecstatic mood, symbolized by the features of the natural scene in the rainy season.

69

The Princess Draupadī of Mahābhārata fame fell into the hands of the Kaurava princes Duryodhana and Duḥśāsana as a result of a gambling-match. When she proudly refused to obey their command to sweep the floor, Duḥśāsana tried to disgrace her by disrobing her in the Assembly. But she called upon the Lord in her plight, and her dress was miraculously lengthened every time he pulled it away.

70

See Note 2.

71

See Note 56.

72

The authorities differ on the meaning of the word harāṃ. I follow Śaśi Prabhā.

73

Release from transmigration. Grammatically a difficult line. I have taken dīśyām to mean "dikhā diyā" and "moccha-nevāj" as a kind of bahuvrīhi compound meaning "One who compassionately dispenses release."

74

Adopting the reading pej for lāj.

75

On Rām, see Note 30. The "Sant" interpretation could be relevant here.

76

See Note 57.

77

Or : "He neither removed my veil nor spoke." There are no pronouns, and the commentators differ.

78

Literally "Rāma". But see Note 30.

79

See Note 29.

80

More literally : "Not the one who loses it." The exact meaning of the line seems uncertain, but it has been taken as a bitter reproach to the Lord.

81

The commentators differ over the meaning of the final sentence.

82

Bābul = bābā = father. According to the generally accepted view of Mīrā's life, she saw little of her father when she was grown up. Unless it were to be taken as a memory of her early childhood, the reference would apparently either have to be to Dūdā jī, Rāṇā Sāṅgā or Vīram Deva. It is a most awkward line. Could it be a merely *imagined* situation ?

83

Reading karad for darad with D. S. Bhāṭī.

84

The cātaka bird (Indian cuckoo) is fabled to drink only that water which has fallen when the moon is in the constellation of Svāti and to spurn all other water.

85

Reading pīva pīva for pīla with Śaśi Prabhā. The bird's natural call is taken to be a repetition of the word "pīva" meaning "Beloved" or "Darling' as she waits faithfully for her "lover", the rain-cloud that appears at the time when the moon is passing through the constellation of Svāti. This call to the Beloved reminds Mīrā agonizingly of her absent Lord.

86

The authorities are not agreed on the exact meaning of the last phrase.

87

Holī is the well-known spring festival in which the Hindus of northern India douche each other with coloured water and apply coloured powder to each other's foreheads, amid much mirth and frolicsome rejoicing.

88

See Note 29.

89

A name of Kṛṣṇa, apparently arising from the fact that he was born in the Yādava tribe, descended from a certain Madhu.

90

tārī = tumhārī : (Śaśi Prabhā)

91

I follow Śaśi Prabhā in taking purāvāṃ as first person singular, not third. On the other interpretation the line would mean that Kṛṣṇa was undergoing a bridal ceremony with someone else in distant parts.

92

Cf. Note 87.

93
As the earth blooms at the arrival of the rains, and as husbands normally return home to their families from commercial or other travel in the rainy season, so the Lord should follow custom and return to His faithful and loving "wife" Mīrā.

94
Reading kaḥ rau vair citāryāṃ with Śaśi Prabhā. The papīhā is a species of cuckoo. Its cry of "piu piu" has the same effect as the "pīva" mentioned in Note 85.

95
Literally "a saw".

96
Reading sukha for mukha.

97
Reading bicharyā for picharyā.

98
Reading ghun for dhun.

99
Reading bini for vidhi.

100
Literally "Rāma", but see Note 30.

101
As Note 100.

102
Reading ghar for par.

103
Dutiyan = dūtikā. (Śaśi Prabhā).

104
Reading ṇeh (or neh) for ṇe with D. S. Bhāṭī and Śaśi Prabhā.

105
Reading ṇibhāvāṃ with Śaśi Prabhā.

106
On Nanda, see Note 14.

107
Literally, "without Thee a body is no body." I follow K. D. Śarmā.

108
Literally, "sit (rest) in my navel." Nābhin = nābhi (navel) plus n, locative termination. (Śaśi Prabhā).

109
āṃṭī (deśaja) = śarārat. R. S. Śukla's Bhāṣā Śabda Koṣa.

110
Sat Guru. The Tāntrikas, Nāthas and Sants emphasized the "internal" Guru. Vaudeville, Kabīr, p. 136 f.

111
Literally, "do not absent yourself."

112

If water falls on them in this month, it changes into pearls. So J. T. Platts, p. 691 (under svāti, svātī).

113

A little earlier than Mīrā, the Bangālī Kṛṣṇa-poet Caṇḍīdāsa attributed a similar belief in crows as a good omen of the coming of the Beloved to Rādhā. Cp. H. P. Dvivedī, Madhya-Kālīna Dharma-Sādhanā p. 193. The traditional belief was that the appearance of a crow portended the arrival of the Beloved, but that the abandoned one must say to the crow, "Go away, my beloved is coming." (D. S. Bhāṭī).

113.a

This poem appears to be in the style of a Bārahamāsā, a Rājasthānī folk-song celebrating the distinctive features of the seasons of the year. Padmāvatī, p. 82.

114

The commentators are not agreed over this obscure line.

115

Śeṣa is the serpent with a thousand heads who forms the couch and canopy for Viṣṇu when the latter is at rest between successive world-periods. As he has a thousand heads he also has a thousand tongues and is consequently very eloquent and very wise. Śiva and Śeṣa in their own very different ways are both emblems of wisdom. Yet Mīrā's Jogī (Kṛṣṇa) is so supremely wise that even Śiva and Śeṣa are happy to meditate on Him, for inspiration.

116

"ṇ" is here not a negative but a jussive particle. (Śaśi Prabhā).

116.a

On ḍignā as "to shudder", cp. Tulasīdāsa, Kavitāvalī I.11, quoted in Tulasī Śabda Sāgara, ḍigati urvi ati gurvi.

117

On Ahilyā, see Note 5. The Lord touched the stone statue of Ahilyā, and Ahilyā's body recovered its beauty and was transported to the skies. If the Lord could raise a whole stone statue to the skies, surely He could easily raise up Mīrā, wasting away and thin as a rake.

118

The authorities are not agreed on the meaning of this obscure phrase. I follow K. D. Śarmā. The Sūra Kośa and Tulasī Śabda Sāgara support "śobhā denā" as the meaning of "chājnā".

119

Another obscure phrase. I follow Śaśi Prabhā in taking balihāriyai as an imperative.

120

Reading "chau" (you are) plus "jī".

121

Literally, "the world knows."

122
Dr. Śaśi Prabhā avoids all reference to the "anhad" music here, and I follow her in this.

123
Mīrā here calls upon Kṛṣṇa as "Giridhara Govardhana", two names having the same meaning. See Note 8.

124
I.e. Draupadī, see Note 69.

125
According to the Vaiṣṇava traditions, the demons called Daityas stole the Vedas from the gods at the beginning of the world-period and Viṣṇu assumed the form of a horse (haya) or horse-necked creature (haya-grīva) and slew the Daityas and recovered the Vedas for the benefit of the gods. There are various forms of the legend.

126
Or "my Master". Sitarāj=Persian sar-tāj.

127
A list of names is given by Y. Śarmā and T. Ṭaṇḍan in their ṭīkā. But the line need not necessarily be taken as evidence that Mīrā visited distant parts of South India. It could well be just a vague indication that she visited many places of pilgrimage, or even a mere assertion that even if she had done so she would have returned empty. The phrase occurs also in Poem 30.

128
Ajāmila was a fallen Brahmin whose sins were erased and who was transported to the abode of Viṣṇu simply because he called for his son on his death-bed and his son's name happened to be Nārāyaṇa. Such is the power of the holy Name of God.

129
Sadanā was a devotee of Viṣṇu who plied the (in a Hindu's eyes) degrading trade of a butcher. It happened that one of the weights he used came from the Śālagrāma stone. (see Note 50) A holy man recognized it and took it away to worship it, but was instructed in a dream to return it. When Sadanā heard of this, he gave up his tradc and went to Bhuvaneśvara as a wandering beggar. Eventually he obtained release. His case is often cited by the Bhaktas to show that it is internal piety and goodness that count in attracting the grace of the Lord and not the external circumstances.

130
See Note 56.

131
The courtesan Jīvantī lacked a child and acquired a pet parrot as a substitute. She taught it to say the Name of God "Rāma", and together they would repeat it. At her death she and the parrot were transported by aerial chariot to the realm of Viṣṇu. Such is the purifying effect of the repetition of the Name of God.

132

The hunchback woman was a devotee of Kṛṣṇa who served at the court of King Kaṃsa in Mathurā. Kṛṣṇa miraculously straightened her body. For the wild woman of the woods, see Note 144 and Poem 186.

133

Some of the commentators enumerate the eight "bonds" mentioned in the Kulārṇava Tantra, hatred, shame, fear, doubt, disgust, family-convention, individual disposition and caste-custom. The list fits the context, but one may doubt if Mīrā took inspiration directly from Tāntrika sources.

134

Reading varyāṃ for vasyāṃ.

135

See Note 56.

136

See Note 69.

137

See Note 2.

138

i.e. Ahilyā, wife of Rishi Gautama. See Notes 5 and 117.

139

Sudāmā, Kṛṣṇa's boyhood friend, fell upon evil days in later life, and went to see Kṛṣṇa, taking as a present a few grains of rice that his wife had managed to save with the greatest difficulty. Kṛṣṇa accepted the gift joyously and later heaped great wealth on Sudāmā.

140

According to tradition, Kabīr, the renowned mystic, gave away all the cloth he had woven in the bazaar, down to the very clothes he was wearing, and did not dare to go back home to his family naked and empty-handed. But the Lord assumed the form of a rich merchant and took an ox laden with provisions to Kabīr's home.

141

It is said that the house of the saint Nāma Deva caught fire. As the saint worshipped God in everything, he took the opportunity to worship Him in the fire, into which he made an offering of his other belongings ! The Lord, pleased with this resignation, personally attended to the mending of the saint's roof that night.

142

The saint Dhannā was a farmer. One day he set off to plough but gave away all his seed to feed the holy men and then ploughed his field without seed, as he was embarassed to return to his family without having ploughed. Later the field sprouted miraculously.

143

See Note 56.

144

The wild woman of the forest, Śabarī, had nothing but plums to offer the avatāra Rāma. She bit into them to pick out the ripe ones, but Rāma accepted the gift gladly and ate the soiled plums.

145

See Note 139.

146

Karamā Bāī lived in Jagannātha Purī and offered the Lord milk and rice with devotion. Eventually He assumed the form of a child and came to eat it in her house. A holy man informed Karamā Bāī that she was not observing the proper ritual before cooking. The next day she was late with the milk and rice as she had been busy with the ritual. When the priests threw open the temple gates that morning they saw the remains of food round the lips of the image. The deity explained by means of a voice from the sky that Karamā Bāī was late with the food and He had had to hurry eating it. The point of the tradition is that the Lord cares more for offerings made with a loving heart than for meticulous performance of ritual.

147

The commentators are divided over the meaning of this obscure phrase. I follow Y. Śarmā and T. Ṭaṇḍan, who agree with Śaśi Prabhā in taking pāṇī to mean water. If pāṇī meant prāṇī (as it does for K. D. Śarmā and D. S. Bhāṭī) the meaning would be something like "The whole world is saved, from stones (like Ahilyā) to living creatures." This interpretation, though not here adopted, is defensible. Cp. Tulasīdāsa, Vinaya Patrikā 257, pāhana, pasu, pataṅga, kola, bhīla, nisicara/kāṃca te kṛpānidhāna kiye subaraṇa.

148

On the courtesan, see Note 131; on the elephant Note 56, on Ajāmila Note 128. Garuḍa, the vehicle of Viṣṇu, has a body half like a man and half like an eagle with brilliant plumage. He is personified as an ideal devotee. Originally he was the sun, conceived in Vedic times as a marvellous bird and in the Purāṇas as a servant of Viṣṇu.

149

Reading jaga for gaja.

150

Viṭṭhala Nātha is now usually held to have been originally a local deity, who came to be worshipped as Kṛṣṇa in company with His spouse Rukmiṇī in the temple of Paṇḍharpur, some 200 miles south-east of Bombay. Already some centuries before Mīrā's birth, the devotees of Viṭṭhala Nātha constituted a pious sect of Viṣṇu-worshippers. Great Teachers had already appeared, such as the author of the famous Jñāneśvarī Commentary on the Gītā, and Nāma Deva, who has already been mentioned in Poem 139. (see Note 141) The latter appears to have travelled north and composed some hymns in Hindī as well as the hymns in his native Marāṭhī. The teachings of this school were broadly similar to those of Mīrā, so there is no incongruity in finding a reference to Viṭṭhala Nātha in her works. What distinguishes Mīrābāī from the Kṛṣṇa poets of other schools and unites her with that of Jñāneśvara is her refusal to draw any firm distinction between worship of the Lord with form and worship of the formless. P. Caturvedī, Bhakti *Sāhitya* meṃ Madhuropāsanā, p. 82. K. D. Śarmā *(p. 17) is surely right* to remark that the reference is not *to Viṭṭhala,* the Guru of Raidāsa's school.

151

The translator is unsure of the meaning of citta-mālā. It has been taken as meant to suggest the continuous revolving of thoughts in the mind like the continuous revolving of the beads of a rosary. Citta=man meṃ. (Śaśi Prabhā).

152

Names of Viṣṇu, who is nevertheless predominantly conceived as Kṛṣṇa by Mīrā.

153

A conception which has also appeared in Poems 84 and 101, and which goes back to the oldest prose Upanishads, notably Bṛhadāraṇyaka Upan. III.vii.1.

154

Puruṣottama, cp. Bhagavad Gītā X.15, XI.3, XV.18 and 19 etc.

155

Another name for Viṣṇu, referring to the fact that He bestrode the universe in three strides.

156

Literally, "There is no under-garment." A perplexing phrase because, if taken literally, it seems to conflict with the first half of the sentence. I follow Y. Śarmā and T. Ṭaṇḍan in softening and generalizing the meaning. Mīrā offers herself mind, body and soul to Kṛṣṇa as a bride offers herself to her husband.

157

Indra is Jupiter Pluvius, the god of rain.

158

The commentators take the "five companions" of the text as the five senses. But the term "five" was also used to mean "some", and the literal meaning of sakhyāṃ seems to yield the better sense. Compare Poem 174 below, and also Tulasīdāsa's Rāma Carita Mānasa II.xxiv.1, mili dasa pāṃca rāma pahiṃ jāhīṃ.

159

The rite is associated with thoughts of the husband. "Maidens worship Gouri and invoke Her grace and blessings for securing a suitable bridegroom. She is adored by married women also for securing long life for their husbands." Svāmī Śivānanda, p. 128.

160

On Holī, see Note 87. There are obviously elements of symbolism in the poem. The poet's soul, dyed in the love of Kṛṣṇa, is evoked by the mention of the dyed water used in the Holī festival and so forth.

161

Sājāṃ is taken to mean susajjita hai. Literally, "Every limb of my body is decorated with joy."

162

Sitarāj=sar-tāj, literally "my crown"

163

Literally, "the crown of (amongst) men of good taste."

164

Literally, "Either my dearest Beloved knows my pain or else I do."

165

K. D. Śarmā very appositely quotes from Kabīr's Granthāvalī, Dohā section, Niguṇāṃ kau aṅga, "Kabīr hari rasa barakhiyā etc." "Water collects in low ground, not on mountain-tops." The quotation supports Dr. Śarmā's contention that the present poem was composed under the influence of Sant teaching.

166

Kara=kara liyā. (Śaśi Prabhā) The present poem is difficult to interpret. There are practically no pronouns, and the commentators are divided on the question whether the strictures it contains are addressed to Mīrā herself or to others. In the present translation, the clearly expressed "me" (mohiṃ) of "has bound me with the cord of greed" has been taken to set the tone of the whole poem. This follows Y. N. Śarmā and T. Ṭaṇḍan.

167

Phiryā=phirī (fem.) (Śaśi Prabhā)

168

The elder brother of Kṛṣṇa, brought up with Him in the family of Nanda at Gokula.

169

The serpent Kāliya, cp. Note 6. There are various forms of the legend.

170

Dr. Śaśi Prabhā records baiṭhī as a feminine form here, according to which it would have to be the sāṛī that was "sitting on the branch of a tree," subsequently to be removed from it by Kṛṣṇa. All the previous translations consulted, however, put Kṛṣṇa Himself on the branch of the tree, which agrees with Śrīmad Bhāgavata X.xxii.9. (Ramaswami Sastrulu Ed, Madras, Vol. II, p. 1326) It seems to be a doubtful case.

171

Reading "de mohiṃ tārī" in this line and "de mohiṃ gārī" in the following one following D. S. Bhāṭī and also Y. N. Śarmā and T. Ṭaṇḍan.

172

In this and the previous poem Kṛṣna manifests as a mischievous little boy. But in doing so He evokes a response of such simple-hearted love from His devotee that He shows Himself to be a greater "rasika" and "nāgara" than any worldly exponent of the art of love. It is worth remarking that the following line referring to a mother-in-law and a sister-in-law is very probably an interpolation. Mīrā's alleged "sister-in-law" Ūdā is a shadowy figure indeed, and her historical existence has apparently never been proved. Padmāvatī "Śabnam" thinks that she is a mental creation arising from the belief that "Ūdā", the shortened form of "Udayakarṇa", the name of Rāṇā Rāymal's parricide elder borther, had a feminine termination and referred to a woman. (Padmāvatī, p. 172 etc.) But in this context, it seems that the name of Vikramājīta's younger brother Udaya Siṃha could be invoked with equal cogency.

173

Taking "hajārī" to mean a form of chaplet or necklace as at the line quoted by Padmāvatī "Śabnam". (Padmāvatī, p. 6, footnote 5, and p. 85, pahiro hāra hajārī) The line quoted concerns Ūdā and can hardly be by Mīrā. But it seems to provide the best clue to the meaning of "hajārī" in the present context.

174

leṃgo=lūṃgā. (Śaśi Prabhā) It is assumed here that this can be used as a feminine. But the meaning seems obscure throughout the second half of the poem. Each of the three earlier translations consulted takes it differently, and the general absence of pronouns helps to reduce the translator to guesswork. I follow K. D. Śarmā in thinking that in the first few lines Mīrā is speaking about herself; then the subject changes to Rādhā, and finally it returns to Mīrā herself.

175

Gāgara is probably a better reading than nāgara, as the verb hatī is in the feminine. I again follow K. D. Śarmā, as also in attributing the golden pot to Mīrā's head and not to Kṛṣṇa's. The commentators differ here, probably on account of the absence of pronouns.

176

Buddhi=hoś (Śaśi Prabhā) Cp. Poem 87, last line.

177

Gujariyā, strictly a woman of the "Gūjar" caste, an inferior caste of Rājpūts, but by extension a cowherd-maiden generally. (Platts, p. 923, under the heading Gūjar)

178

Literally, "like the moon on the second day of the lunar month."

179

Krūra Akrūra, cruel Akrūra, a play on words. Akrūra was Kṛṣṇa's uncle, sent by the wicked King Kaṃsa to fetch Kṛṣṇa and Balarāma from Bṛndāvana to take part in the games at Mathurā.

180

The friend of Kṛṣṇa, sent by Him from Mathurā to the Gopīs of Bṛndāvana with a letter of consolation.

181

Reading "pahlī jñāna mā nahiṃ kīnhau," where "mā" is taken to mean "O companion" and is dropped in the translation.

182

Literally, "packed the parcel of".

183

Rainām=rāt. (Śaśi Prabhā) The line is somewhat obscure. Apparently Mīrā is vividly imagining herself in the presence of the Lord in Bṛndāvana, even as the Christian saints have vividly imagined themselves in the presence of Christ on the cross.

184

It is reasonable to take the opening lines of this poem as spoken by the Gopīs in chorus. See Note 180.

185

Literally Rāma. But see Note 30. For the elephant, see Note 56.

186

See Note 144.

187

The heaven of Viṣṇu.

188

As at Note 185.

189

See Note 139.

190

Mīrā uses the term bhāvaja (=Sanskrit bhrātṛ-jāyā), of which the familiar modern form is bhābhī. Strictly the term means the wife of an elder brother, but its use is extended in various ways. Here it is used to refer to the wife of a friend so intimate as to regard himself as a brother.

191

Unfortunately, the authorities are not agreed over the force of the key-word"baiṭho" in this obscure verse. I follow the line of K. D. Śarmā, who renders it "I sat". Y. N. Śarmā and T. Ṭaṇḍan render it "you sat", as does Bhuvaneśvara Nātha Miśra (p. 168 f.). Śaśi Prabhā renders it in the imperative, "Be seated".

192

A cloth used to cover the hand in which the rosary is held from view.

193

I.e. as a result of her deeds in previous births.

194

Hariścandra, King of Ayodhyā, was so virtuous that he attracted the envy of Indra, who sent the sage Viśvāmitra to test him. Having first extracted his kingdom as a charitable gift, Viśvāmitra then came begging for money. The King took service as a water-carrier in the house of a low-caste man to earn some money to give to the sage. This was only a small part of his tribulations.

195

At the end of the Mahābhārata, it is recorded how the Pāṇḍava brothers climbed up the Himālayas with their queen, Queen Draupadī, and that the latter was the first to fall.

195a

The demon Bali aimed to oust Indra, king of the gods. But he was tricked by Viṣṇu in the form of the holy Dwarf, and ended up banished to Pātāla, the realm in the nether regions below the earth.

196

See Note 32.

196a

This poem seems to fall into the same class as Nazīr's "Duniyā bhī kyā tamāśā hai," "Nazīr kī Bānī", Ed. "Firāq", Allahabad, 1953, p. 120.

197

According to the poetic convention, the partridge is so much in love with the moon that it swallows burning coals, mistaking them for fragments of the moon.

197a

There seem to be two levels of meaning in this poem. At one level Mīrā is referring to the pure waters of the inmost core of the soul, always present but only to be "reached" by utter detachment from everything external, achieved through meditative practices (sādhanā). But the individual soul that has merged with the supreme Self is known in Indian spiritual tradition as a swan (haṃsa, paramahaṃsa). Cp. Śvetāśvatara Upanishad VI.15. So Mīrā is also apparently addressing the pupil-devotee and saying "Go and associate with the Paramahaṃsas in sat-sang on the highest plane of spiritual detachment." K. D. Śarmā and D. S. Bhāṭī rightly draw attention to the presence of the characteristic imagery of the Sant or Nirguṇa tradition in this poem. References to the "sahaja" state of consciousness as an "inaccessible place" are common to many forms of Tāntrika teaching. Cp. Vaudeville, Kabīr, p. 125. As regards Kabīr, see the references given in the Kabīr Kośa of Paraśurāma Caturvedī and Mahendra under "agama" and "haṃsa".

198

The interpretation is doubtful. "Jugatāṃ" has here been taken to mean "yuktiyāṃ" following Y. N. Śarmā and T. Ṭaṇḍan.

199

I.e. there one may acquire the sixteen kinds of spiritual virtue, which are actually detailed in another familiar version of the poem.

200

Rāma-Nāma. But see Note 30.

201

Reading raṅg for saṅg.

202

Raṇa-choṛ=He who abandoned the battle, a name given to Kṛṣṇa in the vernacular to commemorate the fact that He abandoned the defence of Mathurā when it was attacked by Jarāsandha and retired to Dvāraka. Mīrā is believed to have died in the temple of Raṇa-choṛ at Dvāraka. There is at least some presumption that she lived and worshipped there or in that general locality towards the end of her life.

203

Jhāṃlara=laṭakī huī motiyoṃ kī laṛiyāṃ. (Śaśi Prabhā)

204

A name of Kṛṣṇa which addresses Him as the adolescent son of Nanda.

INDEX OF POEMS

Authorities Quoted

Bhāṭī, D.S. — *Mīrāṃbāī aur un kī Padāvalī*, Delhi, 4th Ed. 1975

Braj Bhāṣā Sūra Kośa — See Gupta, D.D.

Caturvedī, P. — *Mīrāṃbāī kī Padāvalī*, Allahabad, 15th Ed. 1973

Madhya-kālīna Prem-Sādhanā, Allahabad, 3rd Ed. 1962

Bhakti Sāhitya meṃ Madhuropāsanā, Allahabad, 1961

Uttarī Bhārata kī Sant-Paramparā, Allahabad, 1951

Vaiṣṇava Dharma, Delhi, n.d.

De, S.K. — *Aspects of Sanskrit Literature*, Calcutta, 1959

Dvivedī, H.P. — *Madhya-kālīna Dharma-sādhanā*, Allahabad, 2nd Ed. 1956

Kabīr, Bombay, 5th Ed. 1955

Goetz, H. — *Mirabai*, Bombay, 1966

Gonda, J. — *Les Religions de l'Inde*, Vol.II, Paris, 1965

Gupta D.D. and Ṭaṇḍan, P.N. — *Braj Bhāṣā Sūra Kośa*, Lucknow, 2 Vols., 1962

Hacker, P. — *Die Idee der Person im Denken von Vedānta-Philosophen*, in Hinduism, Studia Missionalia XIII, Rome, 1963

Hari, Viyogī — *Sant Sudhā Sāra*, Delhi, 1953

Macauliffe, A. — *The Sikh Religion*, Vol. VI, Delhi (reprint), 1963

Miśra, Bhuvaneśvara Nātha "Mādhava" — *Mīrāṃ Kī Prem-Sādhanā* Patnā, 3rd Ed. 1957

Padmāvatī "Shabnam" — *Mīrām: Vyaktitva aur Kṛtitva*, Banāras, 1973

Platts, J.T. — *A Dictionary of Urdū, Classical Hindī and English*,

	Oxford, 1884, reprinted 1960
ŚARMĀ, K.D.	*Mīrāṃbāī Padāvalī*, Delhi, 1972
ŚARMĀ, Y.N. AND ṬAṆḌAN, T.	*Mīrāṃbāī kī Padāvalī kī Sampūrṇa Ṭīkā*, Lucknow, n.d.
ŚAŚI PRABHĀ	*Mīrāṃ Kośa*, Allahabad, 1974
ŚIVĀNANDA, SVĀMĪ	*Hindu Fasts and Festivals*, Rikhikesh, 1947
ŚUKLA, R.S.	*Bhāṣā Śabda Koṣa*, Allahabad, 1936
TIVĀRĪ, H.	*Tulasī Śabda Sāgara*, Allahabad, 1954
Tulasī Śabda Sāgara	See TIVĀRĪ, H.
VARMĀ, D.	*Hindī Sāhitya*, Vol. II, Allahabad, 1959
VARMĀ, V.	*Sūradāsa*, Allahabad, 3rd Ed. 1959
VAUDEVILLE, CH.	*Kabīr*, Vol. I, Oxford, 1974